WE WATCH THE WAVES

UNRAVELLING THE MYSTERY OF A FATHER'S DEATH

SUSAN RILEY

GREAT PLAINS
PUBLICATIONS

Great Plains Publications
420 – 70 Arthur Street
Winnipeg, MB R3B 1G7
www.greatplains.mb.ca

Great Plains Publications gratefully acknowledges the financial support provided for its
publishing program by the Government of Canada through the Book Publishing Industry
Development Program (BPIDP); the Canada Council for the Arts; as well as the Manitoba
Department of Culture, Heritage and Tourism; and the Manitoba Arts Council.

Design & Typography by Relish Design Studios Ltd.
Printed in Canada by Friesens

CANADIAN CATALOGUING IN PUBLICATION DATA

Main entry under title:

Riley, Susan

We watch the waves: unravelling the mystery of a father's death / Susan Riley.

ISBN 978-1-894283-77-9

1. Riley, Susan.   2. Riley, Susan—Family.   3. Winnipeg (Man.)—Biography.
4. Lawyers—Canada—Biography.   5. Journalists—Canada—Biography.   I. Title

KE416.R54A3 2007   340'.092   C2007-904012-8   KF345.Z9R54 2007

TABLE OF CONTENTS

ACKNOWLEDGMENTS

A lot of people helped me piece together this story. Because some of the themes are still loaded even today and partly to protect their and their families' privacy, I have eliminated some names, using only initials. Those I spoke to knew I was eventually writing a book about getting to know my father, but no one, including myself, knew exactly the form it would take or where the exploration would lead. For that reason, I have tried to be careful about using the names of people who were simply helping me know something about my father. I thank all these people for their honesty and compassionate responses to a daughter's search, especially the veterans of World War II who were so generous with their time and their memories.

I thank friends who read early drafts, especially Maureen Hunter, Üstün Reinart, Johanne Leach, Heather Frayne, Michael Riordan and Marjorie Anderson. They always encouraged me to continue. I thank my family, especially my partner Rhonda and my children Chris and Johanne for their love and understanding during what was not only a time-consuming task of researching and writing but an emotional roller-coaster.

Finally I thank my publisher Great Plains Publications and sensitive and sometimes clairvoyant editor Ingeborg Boyens, for believing the story was worth telling.

PROLOGUE

It's a defining moment when we glance sideways into a distant mirror and note with alarm that we are looking at a reflection of the way we remember one or other of our parents. Eerie as a déjà vu, the feeling is triggered by as slight a movement as a lifted eyebrow, a softening around the eyes, a curl of the lips into a half smile. It can create a sweet remembrance of good times past, recognition of inevitable mortality or an acceptance that we might grow up to be people we do not necessarily admire or remember fondly.

I was towel-drying my hair one day in my mid-fifties when I realized I was seeing my mother's face looking back from the steamed-over glass. It was an image tinged with sadness for me because my mother had drastically changed as she aged from her youthful beauty as Alzheimer's took its toll. I was pleased to look anything like my mother as I remembered her when she was young but that day I worried that I too held the seeds of this dreadful disease.

I wished I could change my most vivid memories of her, the ones that kept returning in nightmares, from the indelible images at the end of her life as a confused shell of a person to some at the beginning, a girl full of talent, hope and dreams. She died when she was sixty-nine but I really lost her when her mind failed in her late fifties. Memories kept returning of my mother's arrival at my bridal shower, drunk and confused, blouse stained, one glove missing. That she couldn't find her keys and had no idea where she had left the car embarrassed me in front of my friends. Now I felt guilt at my shame because her deterioration was the beginning of a disease no one had heard of back in the sixties. As I stared into the mirror that morning, I wished I could shift my focus from sadness about how her life ended to the joy I was sure there must have been in her early years. But how could I do this fifteen years after her death, I wondered.

At the same time, I thought about how distressing it was that I could never experience memories or dream any dreams about my father. Other than his likeness in a few photographs, I really had no idea what he looked like. And even those black and white images ended at age thirty-one, when he died. His face would never be aged, it would never even look as old as I did then, myself in middle age with wrinkles, fading freckles and greying hair. Not only did I not remember him but I had never seen a colour photo of him or a moving picture. I remember being surprised during the formation of this book that I could not even find out whether he had been left or right handed. Why should anyone know fifty years later?

Physical likeness to an ancestor is part of the security of knowing where we come from, something of the past to create a sense of belonging. It's comforting to look like someone in the family, an aunt, a sister or a parent. I wanted to know what my father looked like, whether his hair was curly, whether he had a mole on his forearm, whether the skin around his eyes crinkled when he laughed. But, more than that, I wanted to know what he felt, what he thought, what he dreamed and imagined and what made him laugh and cry. I wanted to know if I was at all like him.

When my father died, because of the circumstances around his death, a silence was cast over those around him, an ominous silence threatening to my older brother and me as children. People, both in and outside the family, did not talk freely about him: the mere mention of his name could bring sudden tears to my mother's eyes. He was not a real person in the stories we were told. We were presented with a sanitized picture of a doctor who had been a war hero. He had no faults, not even any annoying habits. The ever-present photograph on the piano when we were little was of a smiling Bill Riley in his Royal Canadian Air Force uniform. I remember staring into those eyes shaded by the peak of an RCAF hat trying to make them come alive. But I only did this when I was alone; I would never have wanted anyone to catch me dwelling on his memory. To us, he was a mysterious, forbidden figure, not available to us.

Researching and writing this book has changed all that for me. Bill Riley is no longer forbidden territory; I am no longer scared to say his name out loud, no longer worried that people around me will be thrown into embarrassed silence when I tell them who my father was. My mother is long dead and his memory no longer haunts her but I do wish she had lived to take this journey with me. I think she would have enjoyed it too, especially watching my brother and me take pleasure in getting to know the man who was our father.

Before she died, my mother had tried to bury his memory, had moved on to a second marriage and a new family. But the shame and taboos surrounding his death in an era without therapy or counselling and in a family of stiff upper lips meant that she bore her grief alone, raised her children in silence and kept painful secrets, even from those closest to her. It's a time—post-war Winnipeg, Manitoba—I try to understand in this book. The Winnipeg of my parents' privileged social class necessarily becomes a character in the story. Perhaps the distance created by a recent move to Vancouver gives me more space to look critically at the city of my earliest memories.

This book, as people who read early versions kept reminding me, is about my journey, my need to recreate the lives of the two young people who were my parents and the forces around them that shaped who they were and what happened to them. It is the story of a detective search some fifty-five years after my father's death when most sources were either very old or dead, a race against the time when the oral history would disappear forever. Fortunately for me, my parents both wrote a lot during their early lives and the family around them preserved the letters and diaries. Their story can never be as interesting to readers as it was to me as I uncovered each surprising twist and turn of their lives. The story I am trying to tell you is also about my own growth during what became, for me, a life-changing search.

The journey is ongoing. It was, after all, not a story to which I could change the ending or supply other answers if I didn't like the ones I was uncovering. Life's journey continues and I find as I grow older that, other than wishing life had been kinder at times, I really do not want to change anything about the story of the two people I have finally come to know as my parents.

Susan Riley, Vancouver, BC
May, 2007

CHAPTER 1

BEGINNINGS

My father died in 1947. I lied to get a copy of the death registration without the "cause of death" blacked out, the way it usually is to discourage the simply curious. It was such a long story to explain to those at a government department that, at age fifty-six, I really didn't know why my father had died. It was just easier to say I needed it for "insurance purposes." The document arrived in the mail a few days later.

The Official Registration of Death recorded that, in the coroner's opinion, the external cause of death was "suicide." Date of injury: *August 24, 1947.* Manner of injury: *revolver bullet through* (a word scratched out) *head.* Nature of injury: *suicide while of unsound mind.*

The cause of death was a chain of events: *cerebral hemorrhage due to lacerated brain due to compound fracture of skull due to bullet wound.* Was there an autopsy? Yes.

It took me months to get a copy of the autopsy report. Everyone I asked said it would have been destroyed long ago, that no one kept records from 1947. Because I had worked as a reporter and a lawyer, I knew it was important to keep trying when officialdom shuts down. Finally, I found a Health Records technician who put me in touch with the right person at Winnipeg's Health Sciences Centre. She was willing to go beyond official channels to help a daughter anxious to find her father's autopsy report from almost sixty years before. She was one of many throughout this journey to take time and effort to help, simply because she cared. "Leave it with me," she said. Two weeks later she called with good news. "I knew the pathology department hangs on to things forever." She had found the original signed autopsy report, still buried in a series of black binders in the pathology department. I had to make a formal access-to-information request but eventually I had a copy.

The Winnipeg General Hospital Autopsy No. 6417 told me in crisp, cold terms about my father's last hours:

> *This man came in from Kenora Sunday night with two companions, arriving in Winnipeg at around 11 pm. This was the last time he was seen alive. He was found Tuesday evening August 26/47 in the basement of his house with a bullet wound in his forehead. A service revolver was in his right hand. It was estimated that he had been dead for 24-36 hours.*

I studied the two-page document carefully. I was later to learn more about the medical terms and their meanings but, at the time, my emotional reaction was profound sadness. There was nothing in the autopsy to explain my father's sudden death, only the stark, physical description of what happens to a skull after a bullet pierces the forehead.

> *The body is that of a young man appearing to be about the stated age of 31 years. Hair is black and curly. The site of entrance of the bullet is at the prominence of the right frontal area.*

The physical findings revealed that, other than the after-effects of the bullet wound, my father was suffering from bronchopneumonia in both lungs, a medical condition but certainly not one that was life threatening. I had been looking for signs of a brain tumor, an incurable illness, a debilitating disease—anything that might make him want to kill himself. Nothing.

The search for the autopsy findings had taken over my life; it had become an end in itself because I was so convinced the report held the answer to why my father killed himself. The autopsy document, when it came, told me how he died but it did not tell me why. It did, however, indicate that what people had been saying was mere speculation and the speculation was wrong: there was no evidence of an incurable illness. His death was now a mystery with no ready explanation and the answer was going to be harder to find, if I could find it at all.

But an important shift had taken place for me, part emotional and part intellectual. This hand-written form, retrieved from its hiding place in piles of archival records, released in me a flood of grief that came with the realization that my father may have chosen to end his life just as mine was beginning. The other reaction was the curiosity that came from all the unanswered questions the new information raised. *If he didn't have an incurable illness, what else was wrong? Was there something hidden in a life that seemed to be full of promise? Had the people around us been hiding something?*

Growing up without a father and being raised by a single mother was a little more unusual in Winnipeg in the 1940s and '50s than it is now but I never thought my life was anything out of the ordinary. I had my mother, my older brother, two sets of grandparents and, later, a step-father. My birth father had been in the war and he had died. That was the story I had been told and there didn't seem anything mysterious about that to me. I grew up with security and confidence, buoyed by my mother's belief that I could do anything. I finished university in Winnipeg and Ottawa and worked as a journalist for newspapers in Toronto and Montreal.

By the early 1970s, I was twenty-five years old and living in Winnipeg with my husband and working at the *Winnipeg Tribune*. It was then that I found out, by accident, that my father had killed himself. The news was shocking, at least partly because it had been kept a secret for so long, although I soon found out that most other people around me when I was growing up, except my brother, had known all along. I readily accepted the trite speculations others offered for the suicide. He had an incurable illness. He had been devastated by the war. Or a combination of the two: he had encountered a deadly disease during his war service and never fully recovered. I was not ready to test any of the stories because it didn't seem to matter much. He was dead, my life was busy, and I could easily concentrate on career and raising children and forget about emotional wounds.

But something else was silently working inside me that I didn't acknowledge then. I saved all the family memorabilia including my mother's diary—in a series of 13 elementary school scribblers, the kind with black shiny covers that produced wavy lines in the light—and her faded green hardcover scrapbook full of newspaper clippings. When my step-father died and we emptied the house, I collected the old letters and diaries, the yellowed stray newspaper clippings, the photograph albums, silver cups from my mother's school days, birth and baptism certificates, report cards tied in bundles with blue ribbon. My father's letters during the war were in the piles, as were many framed portraits of him from his family and the few snapshots my mother kept of their days together. I bought an unfinished trunk with a hinged lid, like a toy box, stained it deep brown, and put these artifacts from my past inside for another day.

I also silently recorded everything I heard about my father. It wasn't much. Few people talked to me about him, but I remembered every snippet of information. Every once in a while, someone would say, when they were introduced to me at a party, "I knew your father during the war" or "I went to school with your father." I didn't follow up at the time but I remembered who these people were and filed their names in the back of my mind, knowing I would go back to them sometime and ask questions: What was he really like? What did he do in the war? What was he like at school and what did you do together?

My mother's death in 1987, after fifteen years with Alzheimer's, finally forced me to stop and reflect. By that time I was 41 and had two teenage children. During her decline, I had begun to blame my father's suicide for my mother's gradual retreat into illness. I thought more about his suicide and the fact that I had never explored what happened. The wondering soon turned into a need to know more about both my parents' lives. I was examining my life, making some major changes, and I thought the story of where I came from might help me understand more about myself. Who was this man who had given me life but then not stayed around for the journey as a parent? Was I like him at all? I knew from his pictures that I had inherited his ears: his protruded under his air force hat the way mine stuck out when I wore my hair back. I wanted and needed to know about him, about what part of me was like him.

But delving into the mystery surrounding my father's death terrified me at first. There was so much I didn't know and people were so uncomfortable talking about him. Friends and relatives always suggested that "digging up the past" would be too difficult and that I should, as they put it, "let it go." It was the need to deal with the grief at my mother's death that propelled me into the search in a backward way. I decided to begin to explore my parents' past through my mother's life, a subject I found easier than my father's death. The first stage of the journey began in earnest in Winnipeg just after my mother's funeral.

• • •

SEPTEMBER, 1987

Her funeral service was held at Thompson's funeral home on Broadway Avenue, ironically the same place my father's body had been taken for the autopsy forty years before, although I didn't know that at the time. My mother's brother, my uncle Larry, had returned to Vancouver, her sister, my aunt Lois, to Montreal and I was left in Winnipeg trying to remember that my mother had once been strong and active and had laughter in her life.

I sat silently alone in my study in front of the wooden box where I kept the old family things. I wasn't sure what I was looking for, but I knew I needed something from the past to help me deal with my grief. I had thought I had grown to accept the loss of my mother during the decade when she didn't know who I was, but the finality of death hit harder than I expected. I lifted the lid of the box.

The old photographs, held in place by black sticky corners in worn albums, did not seem to help. One just added to the mystery. It was an image of my mother Sheila in shorts and T-shirt, floppy straw hat over windblown hair, struggling along a dock, loaded with sailing gear. The caption underneath: "Sloppy Self." My mother in the summer of 1941 at Camp Kamaji, Minnesota, healthy and laughing.

The photograph offered a sharp contrast to the mother I knew from the last ten years who didn't even recognize the ones she loved. Deep in the mists of Alzheimer's, she became an old woman at fifty-five and died at sixty-nine because her mind could not tell her body to eat.

As I sifted through the letters and photographs, I came to the pictures of Marty, the tennis instructor at Kamaji the year Sheila went south to Minnesota to teach sailing to the daughters of rich Americans. The picture triggered memories of my mother talking about Marty and what seemed to me, as a child, one of the least complicated and happiest times of her life—the summer at Kamaji with Marty. When she talked about it, I remembered none of the awkward holding back—and the tears—there was when she remembered my father. I suddenly wondered if I could find Marty after all these years.

Buried under the piles of photos was Sheila's brown leather address book. In it, she had recorded, in her neat private girls' school handwriting beside my name under the "R's", four different addresses, each scratched out as she followed me from university in Ottawa to different apartments in Toronto and Montreal and then to marriage and Winnipeg. Then I saw what I was searching for, under the "M's": *Dorothy Martin, Stephens College, Columbia, Missouri.* Her friend Marty.

Being a reporter by trade and inclination, it didn't take me long to get the number but I hesitated before dialing. I knew I was digging up relics from the past and I did it with trepidation. What if I didn't like what I found?

The voice said, "Stephens College." I asked for Dorothy Martin.

"Oh, she retired years ago." My disappointment registered before the voice continued.

"But I can give you her number—she just lives over on Hilltop."

My palms were damp as I dialed, taking my first tentative step into the past.

"Hello, I'm looking for Dorothy Martin."

"This is Dorothy Martin."

"This is Sheila O'Grady's daughter calling from Winnipeg, Canada…"

"My land…Susan…"

Marty had seen me only once, thirty-seven years earlier on a trip to Winnipeg when she last saw Sheila. I would have been three. It was in the summer of 1950, and the three of us had already moved in with my Riley grandparents on South Drive after my father's death. But despite the long stretch of time, Marty was warm and friendly and seemingly not that surprised to hear from the daughter of her long-ago friend. If she had been anything but welcoming in that first phone call back in 1987, I feel sure I never would have taken this journey. In subsequent conversations, she taught me to embrace the past, to welcome its contradictions and accept its uncertainties and sorrows. She had done that in her own life, dealing with her own father's early tragic death. Marty was a teacher and she taught me that there was nothing to fear from the truth.

As my friendship with Marty grew over the years after my mother's death, so did my need to know more about my father's suicide and my confidence in pursuing answers. All the time, in the back of my mind hovered the box full of old diaries, letters, clippings and photos. It became time to dig them out again at the age of fifty-six. Because I am a writer, it was safest for me to approach the material in the box as research and try to tell the story of my parents as I found it in the box. Working from what I knew and from their own words in the diaries and letters, I began to recreate the story of my parents' lives, filling the holes with imagination. I soon began to enjoy the process. It was a way to begin to know the father I never remember seeing and to believe that my mother had once known love and joy. At the beginning, I decided the story had to start in August 1947.

CHAPTER 2

THE LAST DAY

AUGUST 24, 1947, KEEWATIN, ONTARIO

E ven if I had been with my parents all the time during that last day, I wouldn't have remembered anything. I was nine months old, sleeping most of the time in one of the airy, pine-lined bedrooms in the cottage.

I know what they looked like from photos of my parents and that pebble beach at Keewatin is etched in my memory as the place Mike and I played every summer when we were growing up. I can imagine my father Bill Riley in the summer of 1947 as a fine-boned slender man with black curly hair. That day in August, he sat on the flat rust-colored rock, took off his shoes and socks and rolled up the bottom of his pants. My brother Michael, aged two-and-a-half, clutched a wooden block fitted with a birch-bark sail and swished it back and forth in the water as he waded up to his chubby knees.

My mother Sheila sat on the dock in her bathing suit hugging her knees and looking across the water at her husband and son. I imagine her thinking that Bill looked tired, and she worried that involving him in her parents' financial problems the night before had been a mistake. No one had actually asked Bill to help but my grandparents had confided that they might have to sell the cottage. My mother knew my dad felt he should try to buy it. But he had just started at the new clinic and the timing was not good. Now it was Sunday and Bill was heading back to Winnipeg so they wouldn't have a chance to talk about it.

Sheila looked to the east towards Kenora. Her sailing instincts quickened as she saw the water darken a shade. A gust lifted tiny waves as it headed towards her son, the kind of gust that would give a sail sudden energy. Sailors called it a cat's paw for its stealth and surprise.

Sheila turned and saw that Bill was looking into the distance, his mind on other things. The puff of wind started a ripple of waves behind Michael's little boat and caught the curve of its sail. Michael lifted his hands dramatically and the sailboat took off. He shrieked in surprise and Bill looked startled. Without a moment's hesitation, Sheila dove in, followed the boat expertly with a smooth crawl stroke and, with one hand, pushed it back against the waves towards her son. Michael grinned and grabbed it out of the water. When Sheila joined them on the shore, Bill took his son's hand and helped him over the rocks. The three of them walked up the path to the cottage to change for dinner.

The family ate at the long oilcloth-covered table in the screened dining room overlooking the lake. Sheila's grandfather, "Skipper" Patton, had built this cottage on the northwestern shore of the Lake of the Woods in 1900 when Keewatin Beach was bush and Winnipeg men with money and a sense of adventure bought land in a place without electric power and accessible only by train. He had left it to my grandmother Elsie O'Grady, his only daughter, offering the opinion that his four sons could fend for themselves in a man's world but that his daughter needed a little help. The cottage was a comfortable place where family could gather in front of the brick fireplace in the living room and pop corn in a screen box with a long handle. Others could watch, sitting on stools made of log slabs with odd pieces of cloth tacked over the top. It was not unusual to seat eighteen for dinner on a Saturday night in summer.

But now the family was worried about losing the cottage. My grandfather, Gerald O'Grady, Elsie's husband, had lost his job. An eastern company had bought the cartage business he was running in Winnipeg and brought in their own top management. Jobs were not easy to find in the post-war Winnipeg economy for a man in his fifties who had to compete with returning veterans. Gerald O'Grady was selling insurance but no one, especially he himself, thought he was any good at it. It gave him an office to go to, but hardly any income. The cottage was an asset they could sell, but no one wanted to contemplate summers without Baracouda, as my great-grandfather the Skipper had named it.

Because Bill and my mother's younger brother Larry had to drive back to Winnipeg for the work week, Elsie served an early dinner that Sunday in late August. My mother's sister Lois and her friend Marg completed the group at the dinner table that evening. They ate meatballs, corn on the cob and baked potatoes and Uncle Larry held me on his knee during dessert—a cake with twenty-four candles. It was Larry's birthday.

After dinner that evening, my father, Uncle Larry and Marg, who also had to be back in Winnipeg for work on Monday, left in my father's car for the three-and-a-half hour drive back to Winnipeg. My mother, my brother Mike and I were to stay at the cottage for the week and my father was to return on Friday after work.

He never came back.

• • •

TUESDAY, AUGUST 26, 1947, WINNIPEG, MANITOBA

J. Herbert Riley was in his office at the Northern Trusts Company on Main Street when the receptionist from the Winnipeg Clinic called. Did he know where his son was? Bill had not shown up for work on Monday or that day and there was no answer at his home. Patients were calling, wondering what happened to their appointments. Herb tried his son's number first and then drove to the house. Bill's car was in the driveway. The doors to the house were locked and no one answered the bell. Herb knocked at front and back doors, peering into the windows and getting increasingly agitated. Silence.

Herb knew that Bill and Sheila and the children had been to Keewatin for the weekend and that there was no phone at the O'Grady camp. He went back to his office to phone Larry O'Grady at the Bay department store where he worked. Herb was now suspecting something was wrong and did not want to alarm his wife Ivy by going home. Larry suggested he call the police and get them to break into the house. "I haven't seen Bill since Sunday night when he dropped us off at home. He seemed fine. The last thing he said was 'see you Friday'," Larry said.

The next call to Larry was from the police. "Meet us at 222 Waverley" was the order. The police questioned Larry about the last time he saw Bill. They took him to the basement and he saw what they had found. Fifty years later he could not erase the memory. The magnitude of what this death would mean in the life of his sister and her two children compounded his horror as he stared at the dead body of his brother-in-law.

Herb Riley asked Larry to go tell Sheila and then bring her back to Winnipeg. Larry began the three-and-a-half hour drive back to Keewatin to get his beloved sister Sheila, nephew Michael and niece Susan. In his mind, he rehearsed over and over what he could say that would minimize the impact of the news he had to bring.

The headline in the Wednesday August 27 *Winnipeg Tribune* under a picture of Dr. William Riley in his air force uniform was "Dr. H. W. Riley dies suddenly in city home." He was described as the only son of Mr. and Mrs. J. H. Riley, 749 South Drive in Fort Garry. The story told of his five years in the air force, two of them in India, and his work as a doctor at Deer Lodge Hospital and the Winnipeg Clinic.

The second last paragraph mentioned his young family:

> *His wife, the former Sheila deCourcy O'Grady, has been vacationing at Keewatin Beach with her parents and will be arriving in Winnipeg this afternoon. Besides his parents and his widow, Dr. Riley is survived by a son Michael, aged 2 ½ and a daughter Susan, aged nine months.*

The funeral was at St. Aidans Church in River Heights on Friday. Shocked friends and relatives gathered and Bill's best friend and mentor in medicine Dr. Lennox (Buzz) B. was a pallbearer.

My brother and I did not go to the funeral. We were left at the house on Waverley Street with Amy, the housekeeper. My mother rode to the church in a limousine with the Rileys, Bill's Aunty Anne, and her own parents. After the service, Sheila turned to Aunty Anne and asked, "How long did you have with your husband?"

"Three and a half years," Aunty Anne replied. Sheila and Bill had been married exactly the same amount of time—to the month. But the two widows, the deaths of their husbands separated by thirty years and two world wars, faced different futures. Sheila had two young children and no way to support them in a society that expected her to stay at home and "be a mother." Aunty Anne had no children and was left a wealthy woman by her father. But they were bonded by their sorrow that day: they had both lost the young men they loved.

CHAPTER 3

YEARS OF SILENCE

For the next seven years, our little family of my mother, my brother and I made our home on the third floor of the Tudor style house at 749 South Drive with my Riley grandparents. This was where my father had grown up in the 1920s. Mine was the bedroom overlooking the front yard. My mother had the room facing south towards the Neal family next door. Mike's bedroom overlooked the back yard and vegetable garden. A small bathroom with tub on curved legs completed our "suite."

My first memories of our life at 749 South Drive are the basic signposts of a happy youth: playing in the asparagus bed dressed in my favorite denim jeans, green corduroy jacket and black rubber boots; watching the butterflies light on flowers, their brightly colored wings glistening like silk in the sun; riding my tricycle around the garden with wooden blocks on the pedals so I could reach them; climbing up on Mr. Smith's egg delivery wagon to pat the horses, dodging coarse tails flicking at flies. I remember the smell of damp oak leaves underfoot in the fall and the sting of prickly caragana hedges when we crouched under them for hide and seek. Mike and I played in the vacant lot next door on the wooden slide and swing set grandfather's handyman had built for our father when he was little. We dug holes in the earth behind the garage trying to reach China and, when we found an old chipped plate in the mud, we cheered that we must be close. We chased the cat through the asparagus bed and we were mystified when her kittens disappeared from the basement and only partly consoled when the adults said she must have hidden them.

One time, one of the Neal boys from next door threw a stone at me as I climbed a tree and I ran to my grandfather crying that I was bleeding.

"He must have thought you were a squirrel," said my grandfather, calmly looking up from his newspaper. I remember knowing that my grandfather did not mean to be unkind but still wishing silently that I had a father who might have been more sympathetic.

Overall, our days as children in our grandparents' house in Fort Garry were filled with happiness and security. My mother was always there and I never remember being worried about being left alone. She was the most beautiful woman I had ever seen. She had a habit of reaching her right hand up to her forehead and coaxing the natural wave in her hair between two fingers, a familiar gesture comforting to me as a child. She was always gentle and patient. My grandparents, Herb and Ivy, were around but not always available to us. My mother would read to us for hours in the morning until we heard the grandparents stirring on the floor below.

One of my earliest memories is of snuggling up in my mother's bed listening to the Coronation of the young Queen Elizabeth. Things British were extremely important to my mother, remnants of the war years when the family had huddled around the radio listening to Churchill's speeches. Royalty moved her and she had compassion for the princess whose father had just died leaving her to do what destiny demanded.

Susie, the live-in maid, had a bedroom down the hall from my grandparents. She was a Baptist and tried to interest us in religious stories, even took us to Church once. But we knew no one else in our family really approved of being a Baptist so we didn't take her church very seriously. She made chocolate chip cookies and golden popovers, baked buns and spread them generously with her own apricot jam. Tommy, the gardener, came several days a week on a bicycle from his home on Jubilee Avenue. He wore a soft tweed cap and showed us worms.

Mike and I walked to school; traffic in Fort Garry in the fifties was not anything to worry about. We explored construction sites as new houses took shape around the original few on South Drive. One new house on the river side of South Drive, called "the Trend House", was open to the public and people filed through it during the day, peering at the modern conveniences from behind rope barricades. The one appliance that interested us was the television set because we had never seen one. We would sit under the ropes and watch Howdy Doody as the crowds filed by. We even watched the black and white test pattern—an image of an Indian head—and discussed whether anything on the screen was moving. One evening, we pried open a basement window of the Trend House and crawled in to watch television after the public display had closed. The police were called when someone noticed the light and my grandfather gave us a lecture about "private property."

The only conflict I can remember from South Drive involved my grandmother. One day we had driven in her Dodge downtown to Eaton's, my mother and I in the back seat. I remember a car door slamming and somehow my grandmother's hand got caught. She was furious and my mother hastily apologized, but I was left thinking it was my fault, maybe because, generally, I was the cause of trouble on those shopping trips to buy clothes for me. Because there were no girls around my age, I always played with boys: my brother and the Neal boys next door. I believed that I should be able to dress like the boys, in jeans, plaid shirts and running shoes. My grandmother, however, expected little girls to wear skirts. On several shopping trips, I refused even to try on the outfits my grandmother had chosen. My mother begged me to at least put on the tartan skirt with the big safety pin on one side so that my grandmother could see what I looked like. I refused and no one could make me.

Some of the other minor struggles involved food. I didn't like vegetables. But well-behaved children in that house were required to eat everything on their plates. I used to wrap my vegetables in my napkin and the hide the soggy bundle under the buffet.

Meals were always formal affairs in the dining room with one grandparent at each end of the oval oak table, Mike and I on opposite sides and my mother beside one of us. Everything was served by Susie who was summoned by a bell that my grandmother operated by pressing her foot on a button hidden under the rug. There were no nicknames in that household. We called them "grandmother" and "grandfather" and my mother called them "Mr. and Mrs. Riley." Our dinners were presided over by a portrait of the bearded family patriarch, my grandfather's father, R.T. Riley, in an ornate gilt frame. He had come to Winnipeg from England in 1881 and built a business empire on hard work and Methodist values, we were told.

Thursday nights were different. It was maid's night out. My grandparents usually went to the country club for dinner and that left the kitchen free for the three of us and my mother sometimes let us cook. We used to make something we called a "what," a mixture of whatever we could find, thrown into a frying pan and burned by my brother, standing on a chair at the stove.

Christmas night was spent with my mother's relatives in Tuxedo, across the city. These were raucous affairs compared to life at South Drive. Uncle Eric would drink too much and Grandfather O'Grady would get angry. Rex would make bunny rabbits out of white handkerchiefs and Mr. R. would recite a long Christmas poem with the name of each guest worked into a verse:

> *We all wish we were Rex Wooton*
> *His life is so high falooten…*

Mike and I would haul out a hockey game with marble pucks and tin players controlled by levers that twirled the players in vain efforts to imitate a slap shot. One frequent guest was Mr. R.'s daughter, an actress from Toronto, whom we watched in a CBC drama one Christmas night. She later achieved a certain fame by being married to Canadian novelist Timothy Findley for less than four months. Many years later I learned that Findley was gay and that he had a long-term relationship with a CBC producer and they lived in a big stone house with lots of cats. No one in my family ever talked about her marriage to Timothy Findley or about the cats in the stone house.

I remember in those early years in my grandparents' house, my mother was there to watch us say our prayers before bed, kiss us goodnight and then be up to play quiet games with us when we woke at five or six in the morning. She did some typing for a friend on her portable Royal set up on a card table in her bedroom and she sewed on a treadle sewing machine by the front window, also in her bedroom. I was watching her sew one day when I fell from the radiator and the pencil I was holding pierced my upper lip. Murray M., my godfather and a doctor, made a house call to stitch it up as I sat on the edge of the bathtub screaming, my mother trying to restrain my flailing arms. I had no way of knowing then that "Doctor Murray" was the first man my mother had ever loved.

My father, Bill Riley, was a framed photograph on the grand piano in the living room downstairs. He was wearing his RCAF uniform, ears sticking out from under an airforce hat. I knew three things about him for sure: he had been a doctor; he had been to war; and he had died. At that early age, I connected his death with the war because the war seemed the only bad thing that had happened to him.

But I must have been absorbing something else about my father—a deep emptiness he had left in my mother's life, a wound that had never healed, still raw and tender many years later. My mother and grandparents created a reverence around his name that made me believe that, if he had lived, everything would have been better. I was given a boy doll and I named him Billy to fill the void he left in our lives.

The first time I remember acknowledging out loud I did not have a father was in Grade One when the teacher asked each of us pupils the names of our mother and father. When it was my turn, I said: "My mother is Sheila Riley and my father is dead." The other children gasped and stared at me. The teacher did not know what to say and just moved on to the next pupil. The rest of the day I felt like "the girl without a father," an object for pity because my friends let me go first on the merry-go-round and tried to be especially nice. It was a notoriety I did not enjoy.

My mother spent those seven years socializing with people of another generation. She played a little bridge with the Riley grandparents, their friends and business associates. She spent summers at the cottage at Keewatin with her own parents and, of course, with Mike and me. We were the centre of her world.

While Mike and I both remember those years in Fort Garry as idyllic, it was not until I had children of my own that I started to think about what that time must have been like for my mother. At first one might think she was lucky to have a place to live, meals prepared and gardens tended. But, later in life, I thought about her lack of autonomy. The fact that she was never able to decide what to have for dinner, make a sandwich in her own kitchen or plant a flower in the backyard made me ache for her. And I also had painful recollections of her aloneness. One morning, she had taken us downtown on the bus. At our bus stop on Pembina Highway, she and my brother got off ahead of me. When she turned to lift me down, she realized I was not heavy enough to trigger the automatic door opener. The door closed between us with me still on the bus. The driver went on to the next stop and my terrified mother ran all the way, clutching Mike in her arms. She was breathlessly waiting for me when the bus pulled up at the next stop. Another morning, rushing across her bedroom to turn off the alarm, she tripped over a child's toy and twisted her knee. She lay on the floor, alone and in pain, not wanting to bother my grandparents so early in the morning. I thought how she must have longed for help with the job of parenting or, sometimes, simply for company to share the good times.

Sheila's mother Elsie must have been worried about the pressures on her daughter, for she phoned Marty to ask if she would take Sheila away for a break from the children. Marty had been happy to see her old friend again and the two spent a week at Whitefish Lake, Minnesota swimming, lying on the beach, walking the dog and laughing. When the week was over, Marty drove Sheila north to Canada and delivered her back into the hands of her in-laws Herb and Ivy Riley and her life at 749 South Drive.

"Susan, say hello to Miss Martin. This is the lady who took Mummy away," Grandmother Riley prompted not so helpfully.

"Hello, Susan. I'm Marty, the lady who has brought Mummy back." Marty was never one to back away from a fight and always tried to shift a negative to a positive. Sheila was pretending not to notice the tension between Marty and her mother-in-law, fussing instead with five-year-old Michael. Grandfather Riley, true to his role as peacemaker in that household, diffused the moment by suggesting a drink. Marty asked for bourbon, a big joke because she knew that Canadians usually didn't have any. They settled for rye and water.

Before she left, worried about Sheila living on the top floor of her in-laws' house alone with two children, Marty again repeated her offer. "Come with me. I'll get you at job at Stephens and we can live in my little house nearby. The children can go to school and you can have your own life."

She had made the same offer in a letter two years before when she first learned of Bill's death.

> *I don't know much about children but I have a large back yard where Michael could play—I guess the baby wouldn't be interested just yet. Think it over, Sheila, and if you would like to come for however long, I would be awfully glad.*

Again Sheila said no. "I just couldn't take them away from the Rileys in Winnipeg…it wouldn't be right."

When, many years later, Marty told me that story of meeting my grandparents, she expressed regret that she'd been unable to rescue Sheila from what seemed a lonely life controlled by my grandmother. She thought that Mrs. Riley was critical of my mother and disapproved of her taking even a few days off from parental duties to go to the lake with a friend. When I think about it now, Marty was unconventional and straightforward while my Riley grandparents were proper, conventional and not used to talking about controversy. What they did depended largely on what others in that Winnipeg society approved of. Anything shameful was simply not talked about as if it didn't exist. It makes sense to me now that my grandmother would not have been charmed by Sheila's friend from Missouri, an independent woman with liberal leanings who had supported herself by working as a social worker in the orphanages and prisons of Chicago. But Marty was not governed by what others thought of her. It was exactly that quality that attracted me, and probably my mother, to Marty.

• • •

My mother may have rejected the idea of a dramatic move to the States, but she must have been open to the idea of change as she did date occasionally during those years in Fort Garry. There was no one I particularly remember until the man she married in 1954.

I was in Grade Two when my mother met Murray Old, a bank manager. He bought my brother a fishing rod and tried to be friends with me, but I didn't want to share my mother with anyone. One day, Sheila asked us if she should marry him. I didn't feel that I could say no, especially because my brother was enthusiastic about having a step-dad.

Murray had a daughter a year younger than I and, after the wedding, we all moved into a house in a different part of the city, far away from Fort Garry. We later added Ginger, a nasty little terrier that chased cars and bit their tires.

Bill Riley was not mentioned in the new family and his picture was no longer on display. We still saw our Riley grandparents, usually for Sunday dinner, but no one in our family ever talked to me about my father. When I was twelve, my father's Aunty Anne offered to pay the tuition and I was sent to Balmoral Hall, the private girls' school my mother and both grandmothers had attended. People at my new school would ask me, "Which Riley are you?" It was a confusing question for a child, one without an easy answer. I started by trying to tell them about my mother but, finally, I usually said, "My father was Bill Riley." The reaction was embarrassment or confusion. My best response eventually became, "My mother was Sheila O'Grady." That seemed to satisfy most of them. Either they knew the story of my father's death or they didn't. If they didn't, at least the questions stopped and, if they did, that still ended the conversation. I learned early my father's death wasn't a subject people wanted to pursue with me: it was off limits.

When I was fourteen, one of my friends at Balmoral asked me, "How did your father die?" I replied truthfully that I didn't know. She said, "You should ask your Mum." So I did. One night I approached her in the living room with the question. She was reading a magazine on the overstuffed green couch and, as usual, tears started when she talked about my father.

"He was never the same after he came back from the war," she replied. She probably continued with some story about where he spent the war—in Ceylon and India—and I did not ask further. I naturally avoided the subject, not wanting to upset her any more. Her answer is probably the main reason I thought his death had something to do with the war.

The task of blending two families with infinitely different backgrounds was daunting for Murray and Sheila. Four years after she married Murray, at the age of forty, my mother was pregnant and my half sister Pat was born. By this time, signs of my mother's illness were showing. It began as paranoia, then bouts of drinking too much alcohol, followed by startling memory loss.

Each morning during those years in the late fifties, I travelled across the city to Balmoral Hall. I thrived in the all-female environment where girls could compete without fear of being unpopular. This expensive school offered more enriched academic and sports programs than the public schools I had been attending up to Grade Six. The first summer I was given a "summer reading list," I eagerly devoured all the reading. I made new friends and loved school for the first time. I was elected sports captain and stayed after school every day to supervise games of basketball or volleyball. I spent most of my time at friends' houses across the city and, by Grade Eleven, boarded at school during the week. I was happy to spend less time at home as tensions mounted with my mother's progressing illness.

By the time Mike and I were in university, we were living our own lives and trying to ignore the problems at home. He was developing curling skills that would eventually lead him to world championship play. I was working for grades that would get me accepted into the journalism graduate program at Carleton University in Ottawa. I had virtually no contact with my step-sister and little communication with my half sister, Pat, who was twelve years younger and not even in school yet.

After graduating and working at newspapers in Toronto and Montreal, I returned to Winnipeg to marry a medical student and work as a journalist. I was twenty-five years old and had been married about a year when, one evening, my mother was admitted to hospital after a particularly serious seizure. Her unexplained illness had been progressing and none of the doctors knew what it was. That evening, we had gathered at my stepfather's after visiting her in hospital. We were speculating on what could be wrong with her. "You know," said Murray, "I heard a rumor that her first husband committed suicide. Do you think that could have anything to do with it?"

I fell numb and silent. They continued talking but their voices seemed far away, floating in the air. Inside my head, I was stitching together the bits and pieces I had heard about my father. My step-father's words had shocked me into facing the truth. *That was why my mother had never been able to talk to me about my father, that was why people always avoided the subject of Bill Riley and any mention of his death was vague.* The first jolt of the truth about my father's death was replaced by an urgent need to talk to someone who had known my father. I could think of nothing else. How did he kill himself? Early the next morning, I went to Aunty Anne because I knew she had loved my father like a son. "He shot himself," she confirmed. I didn't ask more. It occurred to me later that, not only had my mother been unable to tell Mike and me how he died but she had also never been able to tell her second husband.

By then, my mother was well-advanced in early onset Alzheimer's but, still, no one knew what was wrong with her. I knew I needed to try to talk to her about my father before it was too late so I went to the hospital with that purpose in mind. She was sitting on the edge of the bed with her legs dangling over the side, a hospital gown tied loosely around her shoulders. Her legs had always been shapely and muscular, the legs of an athlete and dancer, but now they were thin and the shins were white, coloured here and there by greenish bruises where she had bumped into things or fallen. Her greying hair had not been combed but the natural wave at the front was still prominent. She unconsciously kneaded it with her fingers the way I remembered. I sat in the chair in front of her and tried to get her to focus on my father. "I know he killed himself," I said. "Aunty Anne told me." I was crying. My mother had the softest blue eyes, hazy now from the drugs. They also filled with tears. "I couldn't bring myself to tell you. I'm sorry." I wanted most to comfort her, to tell her it was Okay, to tell her it wasn't her fault, to say she had been a great mother. But I said none of those things. I asked her if she knew what happened.

"Just before you came," she said, "I had a dream about Michael. He was walking away from me in the distance, just walking away." I thought this was another of her hallucinations—some were so vivid she tore pictures off the wall in her rage but this one only made her sad. I tried to turn her back to my father. "Why did he do it? Do you know?"

"He was never the same when he came back from the war. But I had no idea…"

She had had years of thinking by herself but had come to no understanding of the reason. She tried to offer me the things that had haunted her.

"At one time I wondered if he had been using drugs but I didn't know what to do. I remember one time the hospital called in the middle of the night. I knew he shouldn't be driving—he was groggy and slurring his speech. He went on the call and I lay awake worrying until I heard the car in the driveway and felt him slip back into bed beside me."

I sat quietly as she talked, hoping that her mind wouldn't wander or her memory disappear. She had never told me anything about their lives together. She paused, thinking of any other detail she might share. "I once found a syringe in his drawer," she said. At the time, I thought that it was not that strange for a doctor to have a syringe at home. Her thoughts were drifting and I thought she wasn't going to continue. Then she said, "I don't know how I got through the night after Larry told me he was dead."

It was the only conversation I ever had with my mother about my father's suicide. That seems a bit odd when I look back but, as a child, the subject of my father was so upsetting to her that I did not dare raise it. And, by the time I knew about the suicide when I was twenty-five, she had lost her ability to think clearly and was too confused to give me many details. My brother was also never able to talk to her about it. We were on our own if we were ever to discover anything else about our father's early death.

CHAPTER 4

MYSTERY

My mother's death in 1987 when I was forty-one ushered me into a double quest: in addition to a need to find out what happened to my father I also yearned to know more about my mother's early life, before tragedy changed it forever. Both their lives were now locked away from me but I hoped it was not too late to begin my search. The beginning of this quest was not a conscious one. One small step—like dialing the number to find Marty—led to another. Each contact was a risk, and I was aware that the answers might not be ones I wanted. In the period of silence of my childhood, I didn't press for information about my father's death because I sensed that the answers might be painful. Once I knew about his suicide, I tried to bury the idea and move on, but his death always hovered in my thoughts. I wrote a story for *Weekend Magazine* about how insurance companies had changed their policies about not paying after a suicide. I wondered if my father had had insurance. But I was still unable to ask direct questions of the people I knew: I was still ashamed and feared what I might find out. I remembered sitting in the car with my mother one day listening to the radio when I was a teenager. A professor from Johns Hopkins University in Baltimore was being interviewed. My mother said, "Your father wanted to go to Johns Hopkins after the war."

"Why didn't he?" I asked.

"Children came along and he was too busy," she answered.

The story had no effect on me at the time but it was one of those bits I stored away, and it came back to me after I learned he killed himself. *What if he didn't want children? What if he didn't want me? Did he feel trapped?* This was speculation I didn't want confirmed.

Finding out about my mother's life came first: there were fewer taboos and so it was easier to talk to people about her. During my forties, I recreated her young life through my friendship with Marty and the process was also fun and fulfilling for me. Marty helped me mourn my mother's early death and to learn more about her life. She assumed the surrogate mother role I needed at the time.

Searching for an understanding of my father took much longer. I pursued that investigation more tentatively, stepping around the minefields of fear and hurt in my search for the truth about his death. The idea that he could have abandoned his young wife and two children by committing suicide was at first more than I could imagine. His act had changed our lives forever. I hoped I might discover it was murder, that perhaps he had been a double agent in the war and that his subsequent stint in Washington was for debriefing. Or that he had had an inoperable brain tumour, or was ravaged by some tropical disease he had caught in the Far East.

And then there was the accommodation of the violence of his death. In having to think about my father's suicide, I was confronted with the vivid image of him, at the age of thirty-one, holding a gun to his forehead, squeezing the trigger and putting a bullet through his brain. I spent the first twenty-five years of my life with the image of him that I had been given by my mother and my Riley grandparents, that of quiet, gentle doctor who had served admirably in the war. It took me the next twenty-five years, until I was in my fifties, to understand how the two images could be connected.

My father had been dead for fifty-five years before I began seriously to search for the reasons behind his death. By that time I had more freedom and skills—I was divorced, my children were grown up and I was working as a lawyer in Winnipeg. I had also learned more about my mother's past and had been down the joyful path with Marty, which gave me more confidence in taking risks. However, by then the trail was cold.

My brother Mike and I had, over the years, casually looked for more information about his suicide but no one came up with much to help us. We both found that people were reluctant to talk to us about our father, were awkward with the subject of suicide. The one time we made a conscious effort to talk to one of his old friends, it was almost as if he was hiding something and the experience discouraged us from asking anyone else.

Just around the same time I learned of my father's suicide in the early 1970s, Mike had also found out. He had asked Aunty Anne directly how his father had died and she told him, as she had told me. Mike and I talked about it together and we decided to visit his old friend, Dr. Buzz B., by then Dean of Medicine at the University of Manitoba. Dr. B. was a highly respected physician known for his uncanny diagnostic skills. He was worshipped by a generation of medical students and the interns' residence was named in his honour. My father was almost ten years younger but had been Buzz's good friend. Because we knew Buzz B. was best man at our parents' wedding, he seemed a logical place to start in any quest to find out more about our father's death.

Mike found the number and made the phone call. Dr. B. agreed to see us and invited us for an evening drink. It was dark by the time we pulled up in front of a gracious old house on Nassau Street in what used to be fashionable central Winnipeg, now a trendy area of shops and bars called Osborne Village. It looked like a fitting scene for our journey into the past. The house, once certainly grand and elegant, now looked neglected and forlorn, leaves gathering on the steps and window frames in need of paint. We stood side by side on the wide stone steps and I pressed the bell. Dr. B. greeted us cordially and showed us into a drawing room that had seen better days. The worn hardwood floors sloped toward the middle of the room. It seemed that he lived alone, there being no evidence of another person that we could see. We really knew very little about him.

The conversation was awkward at first but we soon turned to the reason we had come—our father's suicide. He began by saying he wasn't sure he knew anything that would help us with the reason for Bill's death. But he did offer one memory—of my parents at a party shortly before Bill died. He said that he noticed Bill was slurring his words. He knew Bill was not a particularly heavy drinker and remembered trying to talk to Sheila about this odd behavior. He said he asked her if she "knew what was going on." She didn't. There was a hint of blame in what he told us, blame of my mother for not doing more. This was the first time I was to detect this blame, but it surfaced later, more blatantly.

Buzz B.'s reaction to our questions was typical of many people we talked to over the years. By this time, the tragedy was history to them. Their lives had gone on and it seemed to us they had not given Bill Riley much thought until we asked. Dr. B. politely tried to speculate but, really, he seemed uncomfortable talking to us about our father. In fact, I remember thinking it odd at the time that he changed the subject as quickly as he could to a memoir he was writing about his father's cottage at Fox Lake. Would I read it, he asked, as I was a writer. I politely took a copy.

The visit to Dr. B. was so unproductive that we gave up pursuing answers for a time. Every once in a while, we would meet someone who had been an acquaintance or colleague of our father's and ask what they knew. Several people we talked to repeated rumors that Bill had malaria during the war. One mentioned dengue, another a brain tumour.

The idea of murder took hold for me when my mother's sister Lois told me that Sheila had never accepted the conclusion that my father's death had been from suicide. She thought there were unexplained details. Bill had left the car in the driveway when they had been in the habit of putting it in the garage. There were Cokes and glasses in the living room. She knew Bill never drank Coke. Crumpled newspapers were strewn all over the living room. Bill had been a neat person and would not have left the room this way. And, there was no note. Sheila simply couldn't believe that Bill would not leave a note, that he would leave her with no explanation.

Each time I found out some new detail, I debated whether I wanted to know more. I was curious about the reason for my father's suicide, but some of what was emerging was painful. I didn't want to know any more about my mother's suffering, especially that she might have been blamed. And yet I continued. Breaking the silence always seemed worth it because, as I learned more, I started to lose the fear of what I might find. One day in 2002, I summoned the nerve to make the formal request for the official registration of death from the Medical Examiners Office. Although I had already been told it was suicide, the stark reality of this black and white document with its official seal in the corner was dramatic. Cause of death was handwritten as *revolver bullet in head* and manner of death was *suicide while of unsound mind*. I was especially interested when I saw that an autopsy had been performed. No one had ever mentioned it. Finding it was a turning point in my search. During the months it took to get it, I became sure it would provide the answer. Surely, there would be early signs of a brain tumor he would have known he had or remains of the malaria that would have eventually killed him.

But the autopsy report just raised more questions. It confirmed that Bill Riley died as a result of a bullet that entered his forehead and lodged itself under the skin at the back of his head. His body revealed no other serious abnormalities. He was a healthy young man, perhaps a bit thin, but showed no signs of the effects of chronic disease. His stomach still contained what was probably the remains of that Sunday dinner at the cottage—corn and potatoes. It emitted a slightly sweet odor in Thompson's Funeral home on Broadway Avenue where the young pathologist had been called that August evening to dissect the body. There was one odd detail. The autopsy recorded a needle mark on the inside of his left elbow.

I recognized the name of the pathologist who conducted the autopsy and wrote the report: Dr. J. C. Wilt was the father of a woman I had known in elementary school. A couple of calls confirmed that Dr. Wilt had died a few years back. I had missed my opportunity to speak to him. I began to realize that, if I was going to find people who held the key to the mystery, I was going to have to move quickly.

Every time I re-read the autopsy findings, that profound sadness I felt the first time I read it returned. His death didn't seem inevitable like the end of a rare illness or random accident. I took the autopsy report to a doctor friend who said that there was nothing abnormal he could see in any of the results. He dismissed the idea of chronic drug use. He pointed out that there was only the one needle mark and it could have been from injecting something or even taking blood. And, he said, with the needles in those days, a drug habit would leave a large number of trace marks. He wondered if there was any sign of recent weight loss, a possible indication of depression. I remembered references in my father's letters home from the war to his slight weight and his assurances to his mother that he was eating properly. I didn't think there had been dramatic weight loss before his death. The official war record later revealed that his weight on enlistment in 1940 was a slight 138 pounds while, on discharge in November 1945, it was 148. And no one else who knew him, even his doctor friends who would presumably recognize the signs, had ever mentioned depression.

The archivist at the Winnipeg Clinic searched for records of my father's short time there. He was mentioned in *The Saga of Doctor Thor*, a biography of the founder of the Clinic Dr. P. H. T. Thorlakson.

> *With the cessation of hostilities on both the European and Asian fronts in the summer of 1945, doctors released from the armed forces became available. A number were invited by Dr. Thorlakson to join the Winnipeg Clinic, resulting in important additions to the professional staff: an allergist Dr. C. H. A. Walton; three internists, Dr. J. M. Kilgour, Dr. H. W. Riley and Dr. Jessie McGeachy; a thoracic surgeon, Dr. M. B. (Pit) Perrin; a neuropsychiatrist, Dr. Gilbert Adamson; and a gastroenterologist, Dr. J. Wendell Macleod. Needless to say, this expansion created a compelling urgency to gain more space. In the autumn of 1945, secure in the knowledge that the money would become available, and without waiting for the completion of the legal niceties, Dr. Thorlakson launched the construction project.*

The Clinic sent me a copy of a paper my father had published in 1940 while a resident at the General Hospital. There were also minutes of scientific meetings held in the evenings during 1945 through 1947. My father was a regular at those meetings as was his friend Buzz B.

My unease with the mystery of the suicide remained and in fact grew the more I learned, especially after reading the autopsy report at age fifty-six. In this next more serious stage of my search, I returned to the wooden toy box full of family things. I re-read my mother's diary in those thirteen black scribblers, a day-by-day account kept almost faithfully from 1936 through 1943. I tackled the various packets of my father's war letters, many preserved by my grandparents and my mother in their original blue airmail envelops. I sorted them chronologically, divided them into time periods, and read them all.

I decided the story of their romance had to begin with the war. I continued constructing my story of their lives and found that the more I learned the more I wanted to know. I was actually enjoying getting to know my parents and my fears began to recede.

CHAPTER 5

BITTERSWEET

JANUARY, 1941

Sheila deCourcy O'Grady looked in the mirror and ran her fingers through wet hair. She put the palm of her hand flat on her forehead and used her thumb to shape the natural wave in the front the way Sara had taught her. Today, I can imagine this gesture vividly because I watched her do it many times later in life as she fixed her hair in front of a mirror. But, this evening in 1941 when she was twenty-two, Sheila was preparing for a date with my father. Bill Riley was due any minute to pick her up. Her diary told me that the O'Grady house on Wardlaw Avenue in central Winnipeg was quiet downstairs and no one else seemed to be around to answer the bell.

Interest in Sheila's date for the evening could have come from any member of that diverse household. Her father Gerald would often quiz young men in abrupt military fashion, making it clear that not just anyone was worthy of his eldest daughter. Or, if he had been drinking, he might complain about left-wing liberals. Sheila's mother Elsie was usually off riding horses, but you never knew when she might appear in old riding gear with bits of straw in her hair. Sara, who had helped with the housework since Sheila and her siblings were all babies, was usually in the kitchen and always curious. Sheila said Sara was more of a mother to them than Elsie, who admitted preferring horses and dogs to children. Larry, the baby of the family, said he had four mothers: Elsie, Sara, and older sisters Sheila and Lois. This, he said, was not a blessing.

Then there was Fisher, Elsie's friend, who had needed a place to live when her mother died, moved in and then just stayed on. She and Elsie played practical jokes on people who didn't find them as funny as the two of them did. Elsie and Fisher wore heavy canvas jackets and went duck hunting with the men. Pictures show Elsie and Fisher leaning on shotguns, proudly surveying a line of dead ducks on the ground.

Any number of dogs might also greet visitors in the downstairs hallway. Right then, there was "dear dog," or Patrick, Elsie's elegant black and white English setter and his sidekick Jackie, the cocker spaniel Sheila had won in a Great-West Life raffle. Elsie had immediately said, "You can't keep her. We already have a dog," as if that explained anything. But Sara took the brokenhearted Sheila aside and told her how to deal with Elsie. "Let her pat the puppy once before bed. Then let her feed it. Tomorrow let her hold it." When Jackie was safely snuggled in Elsie's arms the next day, Sara and Sheila shared a smile. Elsie had the last laugh: she had wanted to keep the little dog from the moment she saw her.

Any one of these people or animals could intercept Sheila's dates at the door and usually did. But, tonight, when the doorbell rang, Sheila rushed downstairs and no one else, human or canine, appeared so she and Bill were spared inspections and idle chat, and could leave quickly.

Sheila's diary described the date in detail. When I first read it, I remember feeling very lucky: not many people have a detailed description of the night their parents became engaged. They drove downtown to Moore's Restaurant across from what was then Eaton's for dinner. I later learned from a radio documentary that Moore's was the place to go for aspiring intellectuals and artists. University students liked to lounge in the big leather chairs and soak up the atmosphere. And it was right across the street from the Metropolitan Theatre. That's where Sheila and Bill went after dinner.

The movie was *Bittersweet* with Jeanette Macdonald and Nelson Eddy. Near the beginning and not in reaction to anything particularly romantic on the screen, Bill took her hand. Sheila was pleased and responded by pressing his but it did occur to her that his move was uncharacteristic. Bill Riley was a serious, reserved person and not in the habit of displaying romantic tendencies, particularly in public.

By this time, Sheila and Bill had been going out together on and off for three years. Bill first appeared in Sheila's diary as her friend

Eleanor Riley's older brother. He was mentioned in passing as being present, along with a list of others, at various social events. But I couldn't help noticing that the real excitement in the diary erupted when Murray M. called, not Bill Riley. She even talked about her passion for Murray M. and how she had to fight it because long-lasting relationships, in her mind, were *built on reason, not passion.*

I knew Murray M. as my father's good friend from university days who, after the war, became my godfather and the pediatrician who looked after my brother and me when we were children. We called him "Dr. Murray."

Towards the end of 1939, her diary recorded that Sheila attended a coming-out dance for several of her friends from Rupertsland Girls' School (which later merged with another private girls' school to become the one I attended, Balmoral Hall). She and Eleanor both had dates and so did Bill. They all started off the evening at a *hilarious cocktail party* and then arrived at the dance *a little late for the receiving line.* At 2:30 in the morning, the group, including Bill and Sheila, *staggered into the Salisbury House for coffee.* Sheila said she should never have had coffee because she didn't get to sleep until after five.

The gradual process of getting to know Bill was not one filled either with anxiety or passion. To me, reading about it many years later, the course of their relationship seemed relaxed and natural. They took long drives and drank coffee back at Wardlaw Avenue late into the night. After an evening together, my mother wrote that *Bill is a grand kid and we really did have a lot of fun.* She said she loved talking to him and admired him greatly. There was, however, I noticed, a feeling of discomfort that some of his friends were a little older and, maybe, more sophisticated. Sometimes Sheila said she felt out of place with them. They went to medical parties together, many at Buzz B.'s flat. Buzz was much older than Bill and his friends were other doctors and professors at the university, not students like Bill and Sheila. After one party, Sheila commented that she felt awkward when everyone was happily drinking too much and trying to convince her to do the same.

In September 1939, war was declared. Bill was in his last year of medicine and Sheila was in Arts at the University of Manitoba. Bill began to appear more often in her diary, I noticed. They started going to cocktail parties and dances together even though she was still dating others and pining for Murray M. One afternoon in December, Bill picked her up in the afternoon and they went to see a Trans Canada Airways plane take off at the airfield. Then they went to the General Hospital where Bill was a resident and had coffee with his cousin Harriet, also a doctor. Afterwards they went to Buzz B.'s place.

> It was supposedly for a cocktail party but we stayed for dinner—sherry soup, sherry sauce with the lobster and a glass of scotch. I don't know how I did it but I stayed sober (not used to so much). Then we went back to the Psychopathic (?) where Bill's cousin is now living for awhile. Then Bill and I (only an hour late!!) went to D's to play bridge. D. had to be back at the hospital at 11:30 so the party was not late. Bill came in for a while. It was really a full day and a very nice and unexpected one.

So, by the night they saw *Bittersweet* in early 1941, Bill was an important suitor but, still, she seemed to me not to be aware of how serious he had become. After the movie, they went back to Wardlaw Avenue for coffee. The others were in bed and Sheila and Bill had the kitchen to themselves.

"Sheila," he said, placing his mug carefully in front of him on the table and looking into her eyes, "I love you and I want you to marry me." He was twenty-four and she was twenty-two. He had enlisted in June the year before and was stationed in Toronto. He was home in Winnipeg on leave for only six days.

"I love you, Bill but I'm scared," she replied honestly. "This war is making everyone crazy. I'm worried you're feeling pressure to do things you might not do."

They talked some more. She admitted that she had once been strongly attracted to his close friend from medicine, Murray M. She agreed that night to wear Bill's Zeta Psi fraternity pin, but they decided to keep this outward sign of official engagement out of sight for now so she pinned it to her slip under her sweater. "That's where it will stay for now," she said as she kissed him goodnight. The next day he gave her his gold Royal Canadian Air Force wings which they agreed she would *wear for everyone's benefit.*

Later that night she wrote in her diary:

> *I only hope it is true love. I have no doubt in my mind that we are alike, that we could have a very happy life together... Oh! Bill I hope I love you enough to be worthy of you. If only you really love me for my own sake as you say you do I think everything is O.K. We'll see.*

Two days later he was gone, on a train back to Toronto to continue his training in aviation medicine. *Goodbye until I don't know when, Bill,* she wrote February 1, 1941. Thinking of some of her friends whose husbands and boyfriends had gone overseas, she said she should feel fortunate there was no indication yet that Bill would go.

Sheila resumed her wartime life in Winnipeg. On the urging of her mother, she took a typing course at Success Business College after graduating in Arts and got a job as a secretary at the Great-West Life Assurance Company. The General Manager of the company was soon quite taken with the attractive young woman and had her transferred to become his own personal executive secretary. She felt herself eminently unqualified but obviously had the qualities Harry Manning wanted. Larry later told me that Harry Manning said he had lots of other girls who could type and take shorthand but they didn't have the grace and charm of Sheila O'Grady.

Although she was now officially engaged to Bill Riley, Sheila continued to date as she had before. She had always had many male admirers and the offers from men wanting to take her to dances continued. Young women were often called on to entertain men in uniform stationed temporarily in Winnipeg, and Sheila was in great demand for these dates. The O'Grady's were surprised at the romance with Bill because there had been so many men in Sheila's life and the one they thought was her choice was Murray M. When she displayed her RCAF wings to some friends, they said in a disappointed tone "but we thought you were pledged to the navy." Murray M. was in the navy.

According to her diary, her life in Winnipeg during the war years was busy. She taught swimming at the YMCA, coached basketball at Sacred Heart Convent and danced for the fledgling Winnipeg Ballet Club on the urging of its founder Gwyneth Lloyd. She played bridge with friends, volunteered at war fund raising events and wrote letters to Bill.

• • •

I had known my mother all my life so her early years were easier to imagine than my father's. Her brother Larry and sister Lois told me stories and her diary actually recorded her moods and emotions. But finding out more about her early life started to change my vision of my mother.

As I pieced together her pre-war story, the portrait that emerged was not the mother I had known growing up. It became clear to me that she had been shattered by my father's death. By the time we knew her as our mother, she was emotionally fragile and always guarding a secret place inside.

Although our early childhood living with our Riley grandparents in Fort Garry had been remarkably happy, I began to realize her life there could not have been. She was lonely, overwhelmed by the task of caring for two young children in a house run by elderly and frail grandparents and she felt guilty. She thought there must have been something she could have done to prevent Bill's suicide.

Many years later, I found Susie, the maid who had arrived at my grandparents' house on South Drive November 7, 1950, the day after my fourth birthday. Susie had come to work for my grandparents from her parents' farm in Minnedosa. Although she was thirty-six, this was her first job in the city. My grandparents became like a family to her and she was devoted to them. My grandmother taught her everything about running that kind of household: how to make popovers and shortbread; how to polish silver; and how to feed the cotton sheets through the steam-belching ironing machine. After my grandfather died, her adoration of "Mrs. Riley" grew and, by the end of my grandmother's life, Susie was sleeping with her to comfort her at night. After my grandmother's death, Susie ran a rooming house in central Winnipeg and cooked and cleaned for her younger sister and a house full of usually single male roomers.

When I met her again, she was about to turn ninety, confined to bed across from the dining room on the main floor of that same rooming house. She lay on her side, her wasting body half covered by a loose sheet as she watched the snow whip against the wooden shingles on the house next door. "Old age isn't golden," she said. "It's tarnished brass." The roles had reversed and her sister, seventeen years younger, was now looking after her older sister. Susie had a few things from the Riley house on South Drive that she wanted me to have: baking pans blackened with use, a dusty orange blanket and a desk lamp she said was made by my father at school.

By this time, Susie had more to say about my father's death. She had been told my father had not been well the summer of 1947. She also said Mrs. Riley thought that, if only Sheila had not gone to the lake and left him alone, this never would have happened. Blame seemed far worse than the silence that I had imagined was the background of my mother's life with her in-laws those seven years.

• • •

The journey into my father's past also changed my view of him. I started the serious part of my search when my father would have been eighty-seven and I was fifty-six. At the beginning, he was a mysterious figure, the portrait on the piano. I began by reading diaries and letters but they soon led to people who knew him. But what happened as I continued surprised me. I experienced a flood of grief as the picture of my father emerged; as I began to get to know him, I felt my loss.

My father's life was more difficult than my mother's to recreate because I had never known him and very few people had even talked about him. From what I knew about him and my grandfather, I started by imagining how he might have told his father he had volunteered to go overseas that night in 1941 in the house on South Drive I knew so well, having grown up in it.

CHAPTER 6

THE GREATEST SHOW ON EARTH

JANUARY, 1941

The day after he and Sheila were quietly betrothed, Bill joined his father in the sunroom, a cozy place facing south where Mike and I later spent many hours on the floor reading the *Free Press* comics, what we called "the funny papers." But, on that frigid evening back in 1941, I can see briquette coals glowing in the fireplace as Herb Riley put down the *New Yorker* he was reading when his son sat down in the wicker chair across from him. Bill was wearing his air force uniform. They both would have remembered a similar Sunday night conversation more than a year earlier when there was no uniform and Bill had calmly told his father he was going to enlist.

That earlier December night back in 1939, my grandfather would have been expecting his son to sign up and so he didn't try to talk him out of his decision. He weakly pointed out that Bill had just started his residency in internal medicine at the General Hospital and that perhaps it was not the best time to interrupt medical training. But the newspapers were full of war news by 1939 and the Rileys in Winnipeg believed, along with many people in the British Commonwealth, that Hitler had to be stopped.

The other reality for both Herb and Bill Riley in that time between the world wars was that the military had played a large part in their family. "Fighting for your country" was an honorable thing to do. Bill had been named Harold William after two uncles, his father's younger brother, Harold Riley, and his mother Ivy's only brother, Will Collum. Harold Riley had been a Brigadier General in the First World War and been awarded a Distinguished Service Order (DSO). Will Collum had died from a sniper's bullet in France in 1917, leaving a young widow, Anne Collum. Aunty Anne never married again and treated Bill and his sister Eleanor like her own children. She would remain a devoted friend to Bill all his life and eventually become the first person to tell both Mike and me of his suicide.

Although Bill applied to the service in January of 1940, his appointment as a resident and teaching fellow at the Winnipeg General Hospital was considered essential and it was not until June that he officially began his service career. In those early days of 1941, Bill had been wearing air force blue for less than a year, but his letters revealed that he was getting impatient. He had spent six months at the aviation training school in Kingston and was then moved to Toronto where he was medical officer in charge of a unit, but still in training. He longed to make a difference in the war, he said. By then it was clear the British were in trouble and that a huge effort would be needed to stop the Germans from rolling across the Channel and conquering the island. Bombing blitzes were common in London and the news the Winnipeg Rileys read from overseas was not good.

Bill told his father, on that wintry Sunday night in January of 1941, that he had volunteered to go overseas.

"There are no guarantees and I don't know when it will happen but I know I want to go," he said. His father had known that this too was inevitable. He had many friends who had already lost sons in the war. He did not want his only son anywhere near the action but, again, he did not argue. Herb Riley was a mild-mannered, self-educated man, intelligent and kind. He had not gone to war himself as his older brothers had: he was the one nominated to stay home and watch over the family business in Winnipeg. As the coals in the fireplace faded and the sky outside darkened, father and son talked of war and tried to make sense of the little they knew about world politics. Herb didn't know that Bill had proposed to Sheila O'Grady the night before.

In response to a request from the defence department, Bill later tried to describe a young man's feelings about war service at the time. In an effort to achieve some objectivity he called himself "Joe" and wrote in the third person. It was a tactic he used often in his writing, I noticed later.

It is difficult to state the exact reasons that Joe in January 1940 applied—you had to apply at that time—to join the RCAFMC (Royal Canadian Air Force Medical Corps) attached to the RCAF. Probably the greatest appeal was an emotional one, not to his patriotism but to his spirit of adventure. This might turn out to be the greatest show on earth and here was an opportunity to reserve a ringside seat. There was an element of altruism too, or at any rate, Joe liked to think there was. This war might be important and men might be needed in the future and, if that were so, shouldn't people like Joe, who had had so many advantages, set the example?

In a diary written near the end of 1940, Bill mused about war:

It all started on September 1, 1939—the war I mean. Of course it really began long before that and its roots extend for generations back. But it was on September 1, 1939 that I, and that small world of my generation, had it demonstrated that we were for it...most of us feel that the war and its eventual outcome will shape our individual lives and the lives of the world as a whole inconceivably more than any other single event or series of events in the history of mankind...

I was born in the spring of 1916. The First World War was then two years old and had another two years to run. A few months later, my mother's younger brother was killed overseas, an event which of course made no impression on me then but which nevertheless has influenced my way of thinking to an extent that I am only now beginning to appreciate. Whether he was a remarkable man or not I am really not in a position to say but from the time that I commenced to form my own thoughts I had more or less built him in my imagination as the type of man I wanted to be. My picture of him was not drawn from much that I had heard about him but I had rather endowed him with the qualities that I desired my ideal to possess...

Two of my father's brothers, an older and a younger, were overseas at the same time. The younger brother came back as the young commanding officer of his battalion with a DSO *with two bars to his credit. He is my uncle Harold and my godfather and, though a great soldier, he has as little of the typical military outlook as any man I know. He came back and entered a legal firm in Winnipeg and was latterly a* KC. *Today he is back in harness as District Officer Commanding.*

Reading it many years later, the diary written by a young Bill Riley revealed an amazing sense of duty and responsibility to live up to family heroes, especially wartime ones. It seemed a simpler age when right and wrong appeared more clear.

Bill`s short leave in Winnipeg was over the next day. After seeing him off at the train station, the Rileys invited Sheila O'Grady back to South Drive for dinner, her diary recalled. Herb and Ivy Riley had known Sheila for years as their daughter Eleanor's best friend. Eleanor and Sheila had graduated together from Rupertsland Girls' School where Sheila had been Head Girl in their last year. The Rileys seemed ready to adjust to Sheila's new role as Bill's girlfriend. She was attractive and popular, well-educated and the eldest daughter of a military family. Gerald DeCourcy O'Grady, her father, had been a Colonel in the First World War with the Royal Winnipeg Rifles and wounded twice in action. That night, everyone joked that Sheila was the most important woman at the dinner table because she wore a wing commander's wings while Bill's mother Ivy, Aunty Anne and Eleanor were only attached to air commander-2's. Bill had presented them each smaller wings the night before.

The goodbye at the Winnipeg train station that day was the beginning of a new relationship between my parents by letter. It was a life familiar to many families in wartime Canada. Sheila and Bill's family at home only knew his war by what he chose (or was allowed by censors) to tell them in his letters. The official restrictions played a part, but like many others in action, Bill practiced self-censorship because of concern for those at home. There was no point in telling them the horrors of war;

it would only worry them and could do nothing to change what war was. So the "letters home" tell a story, but not the complete one.

In June, 1941 Bill wrote Sheila from Toronto, reacting to her news that their friend Murray M. had joined the navy:

> I think it is so important that people like Murray who are so much the backbone of this country, should join the services, even though in his case he is sacrificing an excellent training. It should make some of the not-quite-so-fine people think. I was lucky—I had two years of internship and can take up my training any time this job is done but Murray deliberately threw that over.
>
> Ideals are important, aren't they? A reaffirmation of basic ideals is the only thing that will bring this continent to the point where it is doing all that it must do to win the war. So many people still think that personal sacrifice won't be necessary and usually they are the very people who are criticizing the government for its weak-kneed war effort.

This was one of many times when my father showed some concern about life after the war. What would it be like to have to come back and start working again when others had continued with their careers uninterrupted, he wondered. Then he apologized to my mother for his mood.

> I guess I am in a very serious boring mood tonight. I get that way sometimes. Good thing it's not permanent.

And he moved on to her life in Winnipeg without him and her news that she was secretary to the general manager at Great-West Life.

> Your business career was certainly meteoric and I suppose that very soon you will be going to camp. I am so sorry that I won't be able to see you before you go because, oh, my dear, I miss you but its all part of the game.
>
> This is a hell of a letter, my dear—as usual.
>
> Anyway, my love, Bill

• • •

The camp my father referred to in his letter to my mother in June of 1941, was Kamaji in Minnesota where she met Marty. From the time I became immersed in the old letters and diaries, I became especially fascinated with Marty and the time she and my mother spent at camp together. Her letters to my mother were full of life and excitement. They were more passionate and more like love letters than the restrained, proper letters from Bill. The happiest time in my mother's life seemed to be her summer at Camp Kamaji in 1941. After my mother's death and the end of the long bitter Alzheimer's road, it was important for me to recreate the time at camp. It was my attempt to replace my memories of her at the end of her life as a helpless old woman with some of her as a fun-loving young woman. My mother's diary told a lot of the story and I filled in pieces from Marty herself as I got to know her many years later. Their friendship started during the war, in the summer of 1941, just after Sheila and Bill became engaged.

• • •

SUMMER 1941

While Bill was away, my mother continued to date other men. After one date, she wrote in her diary how frustrating it was that, when she wanted to be friends, men so often tried to *make a move*. On this particular occasion, she said she soon put a stop to that and then remarked that a *real friendship with a boy seems fairly hard to work out*. I was fascinated to know that Sheila didn't fall in love with any of these men. In fact, it was clear to me that she didn't fall in love again until she met Marty.

One June evening, she was invited by family friends to a presentation on a camp in the United States that was looking for summer staff. There she was introduced to Miss B. and Miss F., the camp owners. The pair, later to be known as Bert and Phil, were that evening presentably dressed in tailored suits and silk blouses, their recruiting outfits. These would later be replaced by the loose fitting pants and flannel shirts they wore at camp.

By the end of the evening, Sheila was captivated by the moving pictures of Camp Kamaji, in Minnesota. *It was terribly thrilling as I was offered a job for the summer. Though I still can't be sure, I think it is to teach sailing and swimming.*

Elsie offered to drive her down to Minnesota and Larry went along for the ride. They stopped at Crookston for lunch and ate by the river surrounded by tall pines. They found a cabin by Lake Bemidji in Davy's Tourist Camp, slept soundly and cooked their own breakfast before heading for Camp Kamaji early the next morning.

On the first day, Sheila was introduced to the tennis instructor. Dorothy Martin, a social worker who taught sociology at a women's college in Missouri, was at Kamaji for the summer to supplement her teacher's income. Everyone called her Marty. Marty was in her mid-thirties and had been living on her own for over a decade. Sheila had just turned twenty-three and this was her first job away from home. Although their experiences were very different, the two soon discovered they shared the same sense of humour. Bert and Phil, the camp directors, took themselves and their pampered charges seriously and they were not amused when Marty made Sheila laugh during taps the first night. Sheila was embarrassed, but Marty didn't seem to care.

At camp, Sheila found her natural element. She loved the giant log structure with the immense stone fireplace that was the main lodge at Kamaji. She was a competent swimmer, diver and sailor from her summers at Lake of the Woods. She was used to teaching swimming and basketball to children from her part-time jobs and accepted the challenge at camp easily. She showed the campers how to ski Canadian style—on pine needles. But, the most important thing about the summer was the friendship with Marty.

Sheila wrote in her diary in the fall of 1941:

> *Summer at Kamaji this year meant more to me than anything that has ever happened. And I know it was nearly all due to an incomparable friendship with Marty.*

She said she felt more relaxed at camp than she ever did in the city, *less inhibited and less restrained.*

> *I know I am seeing this through rosy coloured glasses because Marty and I found a congeniality, an understanding and almost complete synthesis of viewpoint such as will never be surpassed or probably even equaled. It was a very rare experience; we laughed together until our sides ached, we felt angry together at some signs of injustice or stupidity and we shared a confidence that almost hurt—it was so complete—so satisfactory. It is inexpressible as both of us realize and we lost a lot of our personalities when we separated from the other even for a night. So now that letters are my only solace, I feel very empty—her gift to me of "Testament of Friendship" will continue to warm my heart when I am ninety.*

Marty had enclosed a note in *Testament of Friendship*, the book she sent to Sheila in Winnipeg at the end of August.

> *I think Vera Britain is a very admirable person and sometime you must read her novel "Honorable Estate" and her latest "England's Hour." As I told you, I have my own copy of "Testament of Friendship" and it will afford me a subtle satisfaction to know you have one too! My regret is that we could not have read it together; however we shall talk about it in the not too distant future! There are many reasons that I wanted you to read it aside from its excellence as a book. Perhaps because the title is symbolic or perhaps because it stands out in my mind as one of the most satisfying books I have read—the parallel being obvious since 1941 is in every way an outstanding summer! And right here so much could be said but, suffice it to say, Sheila, that it will forever remain one of those rare experiences never to be repeated. But, to go back to the subject of books, before I digress hopelessly and commit the error of trying to express in words something inexpressible, I can buy books at cost because of my faculty status and would love to send you one from time to time—please don't protest!*

*It would be such a self-indulgence and give me such pleasure...
I have never seen Vera Britain or heard her speak but others say
she is very dynamic and quite attractive. I would imagine all
that and more. Anyhow Sheila the book is a testamonial of a
congeniality which far surpasses any other—ever! And I guess
here would be as good a place as any for you to begin reading
between the lines darling. Just as I predicted, this is a rather long
note—and on glancing back I notice the absence of paragraphs—
but I always say why bother! And since you will be reading
between the lines, paragraphs would be meaningless anyway!*

*And this really deserves a paragraph—I have just realized that
I'm trying rather frantically to say so much when after all I will
be seeing you presently—and there will be many letters so I
needn't attempt to crowd it all into one! But when a person is so
completely filled with a feeling of well-being I suppose it is rather
natural to be verbose. You see darling you have brought it on
yourself, by being so very nice! And according to all rules, since
this "note" was intended to discuss the book primarily, I think I
should add to the coherence of all this by referring to it again,
don't you? Well—my main concern is that you will enjoy it as
much as I did—I know you will and that will be just one more
thing we have in common. The list even now seems endless!*

*Goodbye for the moment my darling—and please be generous
about the inadequacies of this erstwhile note. It's going to be fun
writing to you Sheila—next to talking to you I will like it best
of all things!*

Marty

I know that Marty made at least one trip in her little blue Nash to
Winnipeg and she spent some time with Sheila at the cottage at
Keewatin. Her Winnipeg visit was noted with a picture in the society
pages of the *Free Press*. I found the clipping in my mother's scrapbook. It
was reported that *she was the guest of Mrs. Gerald O'Grady, Wardlaw Ave.
for a short holiday.* She was pictured with Mrs. O'Grady's beautiful setter

Patrick and identified as *Miss Dorothy Martin, PhD., of Stephens College New York.* I knew by the time I read the story that Marty never finished the Ph.D. and Columbia, Missouri was far from New York.

But Marty did meet "dear dog" and the rest of the family. Marty told me they laughed when Elsie returned from walking Patrick complaining that some children had tried to pat him with "their grubby little hands." Elsie's favorite game with Patrick was to walk through the gate of the park and then turn back and watch as Patrick sailed gracefully over the fence to join her. Onlookers were amazed at "dear dog."

Marty and Sheila got caught in the rain and stripped to their slips in the front hall, giggling. They called each other "Sug," short for the Missourian endearment, "Sugar." At the cottage at Keewatin they ate popcorn in front of the fire and played Chinese checkers on the front veranda. Sheila's younger brother Larry asked them why they were so boring, the diary reported.

That fall, Sheila wrote in her diary that her family was furious with her when she insisted on reading a letter from Marty at the dinner table. She had rushed in from ballet practice and ripped open the letter on the way to the table and could not stop reading to say hello.

> *I can see their point and I was selfishly rude about the whole thing. But it was a heavenly letter, all about her Conference and the student mix-up she had been called in to counsel. She's a lamb; there can never be any higher friendship as far as I am concerned than ours. She's the only person to whom I want to tell everything.*

It was a friendship neither could imagine ever ending. As 1941 drew to a close, Sheila wrote:

> *New Year's Eve with Smitty. My goodness I was bored. I'll admit it must have been my own fault because everyone else was blowing tin whistles and things—but oh! for just one understanding look at Marty. Just to curl up on a sofa and say "Hi, Sug."*
>
> *Bill went to a party tonight too. I wonder if he had fun. He's so many miles away. And Marty is so many miles away. It's a waiting life!*

CHAPTER 7

"WE WATCH THE WAVES"

By now, I felt that I was getting a picture of my parents' lives before the war and, as the war progressed, of my mother's summer at Kamaji and her growing friendship with Marty. But, as my father continued his training in the air force in the summer of 1941, I had nothing but his letters to help me follow his journey. And of course, it was a one-way trip, as I had only his letters—not theirs—to explore the relationships between my dad and his loved ones back home. I opened the wooden box and read the letters again, trying to imagine life for a twenty-five-year-old doctor from Fort Garry, Manitoba, preparing to go overseas to fight the Germans. In their idealism and earnestness, Bill's letters were in dramatic contrast to the unbridled joy in the developing friendship between Marty and Sheila.

Until this journey back into my parents' lives, I had never been interested in military history or the Second World War. But I soon began stopping in bookstores and libraries in the "military history" sections and flipping through books and magazines, looking for anything about the RCAF. *Why was my father in the Shetlands? How did he get to Ceylon? What was the RCAF doing in Ceylon when they were supposed to be fighting the Germans?* I needed a context for the letters: they were only telling me about my father's thoughts and feelings. Context came gradually as I learned more about the war.

The letters from Toronto in the summer of 1941 sounded increasingly restless. Bill was preparing to go overseas and he wrote his father in September that he had made an army will and bought a war bond. The medicine was interesting enough and he wrote about getting into the operating room with a perforated ulcer case.

> *The surgeon down there was very nice to me and appeared to*
> *be quite impressed at my making the diagnosis—one of the*

advantages of having a youthful appearance I guess, because it was a case that would have been unthinkable to miss…The boy is fine now—it was one of those things that really make one glad to be a doctor because he would have been gone in an hour if he hadn't been operated on. We don't get many chances to do things like that.

The news that Bill was heading overseas soon was not a surprise back home. He wrote to Sheila:

I hear that Ed (Bill's best friend from childhood) *has gone to sea which is pretty tough on Jean. I sort of envy him though as it is rather exasperating to be doing a quiet job here when so much is happening overseas.*

He wrote his parents with hints that he was hearing from senior officers about heading for a bomber or fighter squadron, which would be a good job for medical training. The next move was to Halifax.

It is possible I may leave Halifax almost on arrival so if you don't hear from me you may assume I am away. If I can send a "happy birthday" telegram you may take it as "au revoir."

He wrote in August on The Nova Scotian Hotel notepaper:

I came to the supper dance here last night…My turn will probably come very soon and very suddenly and it can't come too soon for me as our camp isn't much of a place and it is deadly doing nothing.

August 27, 1941 he wrote from the Y Depot in Halifax:

Dear Mother: things are starting to happen now and I don't imagine that there will be much more inactivity…You should see me all dressed up in a tin hat and carrying a water bottle and a revolver. It is quite something.

The same day he wrote to Sheila:

I expect by the time you read this that I shall no longer be here as I have been waiting now for about a week for transportation

*and getting quite fed up with the inactivity. However that is at
an end now and the show is really on. It is funny wearing a tin
hat and carrying a revolver which I scarcely know how to
handle...Write to me Sheila and tell me all about yourself and
what you are thinking, my love to you, as always, Bill*

The mention of a revolver was shocking to me as I read the reference
in a casual joking tone in both a letter to his mother and to my mother.
Was this, I wondered, the revolver that had finally killed him, kept
hidden away wrapped in old newspaper and buried at the bottom of a
trunk of old war gear? Did he find it the night he shot himself? Had he
kept ammunition with it? Why didn't he have to turn it in when he
was finally released from the air force in 1945? All these questions ran
through my mind as I listened to my young father describe, trying to be
light-hearted, his first contact with a revolver during the war.

Next, I read a letter, dated September 3, 1941. My father was
suddenly At Sea.

*My dear Mother...well there doesn't seem to be much else to
say and still keep within the rules. You may have gathered that
I am neither flying nor going by submarine tunnel but beyond
that there is little to say. The weather—no, that is not for
discussion. Nor would be the course if I knew it...Sept. 11 the
mail is closing now so it looks as if we are nearing the end of
our voyage.*

In September, to Sheila from At Sea, he wrote a long discourse on
the attractions of steam pudding, explaining that you have to try to be
comic in the U-boat zone.

*I am afraid as usual that my letter is very garbled and reflects a
variety of moods and it scarcely expresses the thoughts that I
would like to get across. I think of you so much Sheila—you
really play a feature part in innumerable day dreams. Take care
of yourself and have fun—do the things you want to do and to
hell with well-meaning advisors, because you will be right...*

I noticed that he apologized for his mood often in the letters, trying to make what little information he could reveal into an interesting story to read. On September 16, 1941, he wrote on Cumberland Hotel stationary from Marble Arch, London:

My dear Mother and all of you,

It is great to be here!…immediately transferred to a train where we sat up all night and got our first glimpse of London as the blackout lifted in the early hours of the morning. The blackout is something almost unbelievable…the amazing thing though is the way everything carries on as if it were broad daylight—railway stations are hives of activity, streets jammed with traffic navigating largely by instinct and sidewalks crowded with silhouettes all of whom apparently know where they are going. London is superb. To see the streets you would never know that there were petrol regulations and all the services—taxis, buses, trains, railways are even busier than ever and absolutely on schedule…there is no doubt about that the bombing has been completely indiscriminate without rhyme or reason and it also appears to be a fact that the bombs seem to have had a predilection for churches and hospitals. They make good landmarks I suppose…I walked from St. Paul's Cathedral to London Bridge and it is pretty grim there—very grim in fact but everyone buzzed about their work as if it were September 1935 but there were no unemployed standing around watching.

From earlier letters I knew that my father had been on a bicycle tour of Europe with a friend after high school. This time, during the war, his glimpse of London was very different. Soon, from the RAF Station, West Kirby Cheshire, he revealed that he now had his orders.

Dear Mother and Dad

…I had reached Aberdeen a couple of days ago returning from two very full weeks of leave in and around London when I was instructed to proceed no further and to come here immediately…

During his leave in London, I learned that Bill visited his parents' old friend Earle Duffin. Duffin appeared in my father's war letters frequently. Sixty years later, I couldn't find anyone who could tell me anything about him. I wondered why my father would have chosen to spend so much time with a man his father's age in a city full of young women looking for men in uniform. The only clue I found was in my great-grandfather's memoirs where he explained Duffin's long association with the Riley family. In 1914, Bill's Uncle Harold and his friend Earle Duffin had gone on a trip to Europe. Just as they were ending their trip, World War I was declared. They tried to sign up in London but were advised to return to Canada and enlist, which they did, together. Duffin was best man at Anne and Will Collum's wedding in 1914 and it may have simply been Bill's idealistic view of the uncles he was named after that drew him to Duffin as he too faced the reality of a world war.

By September 20, 1941, Bill wrote that his new address was "# 413 Squadron RAF" and he was now *somewhere in Scotland*. Thus began the series of letters my father wrote to the folks at home during his active war service overseas. I had a special interest in these, letters saved for over fifty years, long after his death: I was sure they were an important way to get to know the man who was my father and also I thought they might hold a clue to his death. He obviously enjoyed writing and wrote a lot. But I was also learning that war letters are a strange breed of correspondence, especially if they come from combat zones, as my father's did for those two years. They were highly censored—the weather, any description of the base or mention of even routine operations, names and places were among the long list of things he couldn't talk about. He admitted that it was a struggle to write an interesting letter with all the restrictions. But he was able to express his sense of isolation and loneliness. I learned something of his ambitions after the war, his youthful political views and his longing for home. As I soaked up everything I could to get to know him, I couldn't help but look for something that might explain his death. My mother, and later old friends of my father, had always spoken of his war experience as if it was a contributing factor to his suicide. The letters were my window on that forgotten time.

I had never heard of RCAF squadron 413 until I read my father's letters, but I discovered that it still existed in Greenwood, Nova Scotia and a lot had been written about its wartime operations. As my father was writing my mother in June of 1941 from Toronto where he was preparing to go overseas, the new squadron 413 was formed in Stanraer, Scotland, part of the RAF Coastal Command. Its motto: "We Watch the Waves" (Ad Vigilamus Undis) describes the squadron's first job during the war: to escort convoys safely to their destinations and to do survey and spy flights looking for the enemy. The plan in the fall of 1941 was that the squadron would patrol the waters off the coasts of Scotland and Norway looking for German submarines, or U-boats, and protect Allied cargo ships. The best long-range aircraft that could also land on water at that time were the American built Catalinas or "flying boats" and no Canadians were yet trained on "Cats." The new squadron 413 took delivery of its first Cat in July of 1941 and the Americans (technically not in the war yet) lent some pilots to help RAF pilots learn to fly them. The first RCAF Commanding Officer R.G. Briese took over 413 in August and, in his first week, a 413 Cat crashed during a take-off at night in bad weather and five of the seven crew members died. At the time of this tragic accident, I figured out that my father was still At Sea. He arrived in London in mid-September, two days before the new 413 squadron got orders to move to Sullom Voe in the Shetland Islands by the beginning of October.

Many years after I had first read my father's letters, I compared information in them with events described in histories of squadron 413. When my father got his orders, he was in London with his family's old friend Duffin and they were able to talk about his new posting, even though Bill couldn't name it in letters home. Whatever connections the Winnipeg Rileys thought they had at the top of the military brass, they didn't get the young RCAF doctor from Manitoba a cushy posting. I found out that my father was headed for the biggest of the Shetland Islands, in the middle of the ocean between Scotland and German-occupied Norway. His new home in Sullom Voe was at the latitude of southern Alaska and James Bay. It rained 260 days of the year, temperatures were in the low forties (Fahrenheit) and winds often gusted to 80 miles per hour. It didn't sound to me like ideal flying conditions. From this isolated bleak and frozen spot, the young, poorly trained, poorly equipped new squadron of men in their twenties like my father was supposed to make cargo ships safe and conduct survey flights off the coast of Norway.

I discovered that Bill's first posting overseas became a bit of a joke after the war for the airmen who survived it. It was likened to a penal colony with only temporary Nissen huts to keep out the damp, frigid winds. Sullom Voe was pretty well despised by all who served there and most wondered what they had done to deserve such a bleak place. In Bill's first letters home, though, he tried to sound cheerful.

In October, 1941, shortly after he arrived, he wrote to my mother:

> *Dear Sheila, It seems strange to be writing from so far away though actually I suppose there is little practical difference between Toronto and Scotland or Caddy Lake for that matter...I am going to like my life as* M.O. *(Medical Officer) to an operational squadron. Much of my job will be straight psychology which is a big factor in the pilot's life of strain and harrowing experiences. There is a fair amount of ordinary medicine and surgery too, enough to keep one's hand in.*

And on October 10, 1941, from the Shetlands he reported to his parents.

> *Dear Mother and Father,*
>
> *...As you can see I have changed my location and expect to settle in for some time to come. This is really a most amazing place. The appearance is much as I have always imagined the surface of the moon at close quarters. There is not a tree on the island—only miles and miles of rolling peat bogs. Sheep outnumber humans in a proportion of about 5 to 1 so if environment is really very important I may be speaking in a series of baas when I leave here. Do not in your letters mention my location as you will be using my squadron number...reason is, I suppose, that while Jerry knows where we are, he presumably doesn't know who we are...At the time of writing, what little we know of the Russian war sounds very grim— however our newspapers are all a week old.*

I noticed, as I read, that the letters to his father and Aunty Anne were full of attempts to decipher the political backdrop to the war and to speculate on what events might mean in the long term. They also dealt with politics back home and issues like conscription and the popularity of the federal government. His letters to his mother mostly tried to reassure her that he was eating properly and that he was not in danger. But, as their daughter, I looked for anything in my parents' letters to each other during the war that revealed something about their relationship. Because I was acutely aware of my mother's loss and abandonment after his suicide, I craved anything in the letters that showed youthful love for one another. Although I only had one half of the war correspondence (his letters), they helped me believe that my parents had been in love, a love built on a true friendship. The letters between them, once in a while, showed the little misunderstandings that arise in long-distance relationships when the only communication is by letter and there are long delays between replies. But generally their love for one another was evident in this correspondence. Having proof of that eased some of the anguish I felt about what was hard not to think of as my father's "abandonment" of her.

On October 24, 1941 my father wrote her from the Shetlands:

My Dearest Sheila,

I must confess I have reached the mooning stage where I watch each mail for your handwriting. Re joining the army—don't without a commission or you will be stuck in Plum Coulee for the duration…One of the things I do is to go out and meet the incoming aircraft and I have had my first experience of meeting one that never returned. It is not a pleasant experience in any case and some of the lads were quite close friends. They are the people who will be responsible if we win this war and not the bureaucrats who sit at desks quoting the latest Air Ministry order to the effect that airmen will not smoke pipes in public places nor yet those who sit comfortably at home and urge that we launch an offensive invasion. Some of these lads were Canadian who had given up good jobs and left families and they weren't the types who would ever regret it or become bitter about it. Enough of that though...and miss me too—nearly as much as I miss you, Ever your devoted, Bill

Interspersed with references to his affection and longing for Sheila were other accounts of that winter in the Shetlands, especially the terrifying flying conditions the aircrew faced. One pilot wrote, on November 7 of that year, describing his attempts to get an aircraft above the clouds. He opened up to full throttle but the aircraft wouldn't climb, the elevators froze up and, soon, the windscreen was ice-covered and the only way he could see was to stick his head out the window.

On October 27, 1941, Bill described a little of his life as medical officer on an isolated and poorly equipped base.

I have undertaken to organize a Central Flying Rations Store to provide decent meals for aircrews during their operational flights and it is occupying a considerable amount of my time as supplies are hard to obtain. I took my ambulance into Lerwick, the metropolis of the Shetlands, and did some shopping but there is really very little to buy...nothing to see but hills and sheep and the well known ponies...had a letter from Portsmouth from Murray M....hope to spend some leave together...the winter underwear was a good idea—the cold and dampness does penetrate...you will have heard that Wing Commander Briese our late C.O. is missing which was pretty tough luck as he was a real going concern—and I hope still is somewhere. I am managing to work in a fair amount of flying which I very much enjoy...no one could be more cozy than I as I sit by my peat stove writing this letter.

On November 11, 1941 he admitted to my mother that he was often lonely and down, especially contemplating the future.

I find it hard to write an interesting letter from here because in a spot like this life is led to a great extent in retrospect and anticipation. The present is something of a limbo between two worlds. The things that matter are behind and ahead and memories and hopes are what make the world go round.

The above is not meant to sound depressed because life is really not bad but it lacks an immediate objective—until the present interlude is over there seems to be little to strive for and existence feels a little empty. Perhaps that is a decadent philosophy and if you see an answer to it, jack me up. Perhaps I'm just lonely.

As I have probably said before, this is a pretty bleak spot and the climate is far from cheery which makes one feel a long way from home. The squadron is a great collection of lads though, doing a wonderful job and all desperately keen and their keenness is infectious. Albeit that I will be glad when it is over, it is an experience that I wouldn't have missed for anything… Excuse my even worse than usual writing. I am sitting in my room before my stove, writing on my lap.

I am sorry this letter is such a blank. You understand the subjects that must obviously be banned—descriptions of the station, our functions, almost any exciting event that may occur, our daily routine and the weather. I think that covers most of the forbidden topics. I can say that the subject that occupies my mind most of all is you. Lord, Sheila, I could never have believed that it was possible to miss a person so and it's getting worse all the time…the distance between us frightens me sometimes because I don't want you to feel duty bound to me. Damn—that's bad! I know you would tell me if it ever began to feel that way…if this letter sounds depressed, I'm not (good Irish that) Just missing you rather terribly, your devoted Bill

The day my father wrote that letter to my mother was the height of a two-day storm, the worst recorded in the Shetlands since 1901, and, of course, he didn't mention it in his letters home. That day, 413 lost four aircraft at their moorings, two of them simply disappearing completely overnight. The Cats were normally only beached for maintenance and otherwise bobbed in the water on their flat bellies, like boats. In bad weather, the crew—a pilot, a rigger and a fitter—were sent on board to try to keep the plane afloat and they often had to stay there until the storm died. In one storm in December 1941 the crew bailed an aircraft by hand for thirty-six hours.

As I read my father's letters from the Shetlands, I learned from D. J. Baker's A History of 413 Squadron (General Store Publishing House, 1997), that the 413 pilots were sent on secret and sensitive missions that winter. One of those missions cost Commander Briese, my father's first C.O., his life. The crew took off October 22 to take photos around Tromso on the northern coast of Norway. Aircraft "G" never came back and the crew of ten was listed missing. It was the new squadron's first operational loss. Briese's body was washed ashore and is buried in Norway and the rest of the crew remained missing.

These historical details helped me recreate this time of my father's life. Although, as a medical officer, he was not carrying out the dangerous flying missions, he would have been seeing his share of casualties and experiencing the psychological fallout from being surrounded by danger and death at a young age. It would not have been an easy life.

On November 28, 1941, my father wrote to Aunty Anne, trying to figure out what was happening in the bigger picture in the war:

> The station medical officer has gone on leave so I am carrying the station as well as my own squadron. It is quite like old times and time does not hang so heavily…I am amusing myself in my spare time by taking some lessons in Norwegian which I find quite enjoyable…the news from the Middle East is not bad just now. I do think it was a bad mistake to give the campaign such a build-up before it really started. Russia is still holding up remarkably though their position is far from rosy. Here the policy seems to be watchful expectancy.

On December 13, 1941, he reported a welcome package from home:

> Dear Mother and Dad:

> Cigarettes and sweetened cocoa from 89 Eastgate (Aunty Anne's house in Winnipeg)…In view of the widening war

front during the past week I should think that overseas conscription would be almost automatic. When I first came over here I had quite a violent reaction against the idea of overseas conscription largely, I suppose, because there is still a very vocal element here who still regard the so-called Dominions as colonies who should without question dispatch their men anywhere at Britain's behest. However, if the services remain under <u>Canadian</u> control I am all for it...Many of us here are hoping we will have a chance to take a crack at the Japs after our term here has expired.

I have had some experience in a small way of dealing with casualties quickly and am glad to feel occasionally of some real use.

On December 18. 1941, he wrote a Christmas letter to his mother:

Christmas is just a few days away and though we haven't much to work with I think we shall make a pretty good show of it. We are hoping to lay our hands on some turkeys which will be a real treat. Though it perhaps will not be a "merry" season either here or at home, we are all lucky to have the fortifying memories of Christmases past and the sure hope of bright ones in the future. Blackout doesn't end til nearly 10 in the morning and is up again before 4 in the afternoon so our daylight hours are few and nights are long.

He tried to paint a contented, domestic picture of his life on January 11, 1942, in a letter to his family back home.

This is Sunday night in these northern isles and if my writing is bad it is because I am sitting in front of my stove with this pad on my knee getting thoroughly warm and listening to the BBC in the background. I have just finished sewing on a couple of buttons, a domestic performance that I always defer until action becomes an urgent necessity. I have a drawer full of socks that I must tackle some day with a view to the odd bit of mending but until my supply of whole ones disappears I probably will do nothing about it...

> *I haven't much to write about. I went to a New Year's party in* (cut out by censor) *which, while not very exciting, was different anyway.*

The day after the New Year's party, during a night anti-submarine sweep, 413 aircraft "F" hit a wireless mast and sheared off one wing. "F" crashed into the sea but the crew was rescued and brought to shore. Night operations were dangerous because of the difficult terrain and poor landing strip at the base. During storms, the Cat would approach, at 75 knots, a path marked by dinghies with flares aboard and the pilot would hope for the best. If the weather was really bad, a huge ocean ship tried to guide the aircraft with a searchlight as it bounced in on the waves. The sailors would throw ropes to the aircrew and attach them to the nose and wings in a "Y" and the crew had to stay on board until a small boat could bring them safely to shore when the winds subsided.

On January 17, a 413 aircraft returning from a guard patrol crashed into Yell Island and burned, killing seven of the 10 on board. The new 413 Commander, J. C. Scott (called "Scotty" in my father's letters), was sent from Sullom Voe to the crash scene and he had to stay seven days until a boat could get in to rescue the injured crew members. The stories of operations that winter showed me the kind of casualties my father as M.O. would have been dealing with back at the base. His letters could not tell the details but one of the operations brought him together with his old friend from medical school, Sheila's first love and my godfather, Murray M. who was in the Navy.

On January 18, 1942, Bill wrote to his mother of the reunion, hinting that the circumstances of the meeting were dangerous:

> *...Murray and I have met and spent a few hours together...the circumstances of our meeting were quite dramatic when one thinks back on how close our association has been in the past five years... We were both so excited and amazed that I think we were the two happiest boys in the world for the short reunion we had, even though there was a pretty dark cloud of uncertainty hanging over us, which is not yet over...*

He also wrote to Sheila, revealing more of his feelings than he did to his mother:

Dear Sheila:

Nothing very startling since my last letter…I suspect that mother tends to dwell on my absence in this spot a little too much with absolutely no real reason…

I forgot the most exciting news of all. I have seen Murray and spent quite a bit of time with him. We have really had glorious times together just discussing old days, in which you figured prominently.

Sometimes my letters may have and may in the future seem a little depressed. It really isn't so, Sheila, so don't let it get you down. It is just a symptom that occasionally develops in people in a remote spot such as this and it doesn't mean a thing. It's what we call getting "bushed" in northern Canada. What I am driving at is this. I don't and haven't ever felt that our interest in each other could ever degenerate into a "duty", in spite of however poorly I have expressed myself. Of course we will always be spontaneous—never forced. If it ever got to be a duty, both of us would say so honestly right away. But it never will. In other words, my darling, I love you very much—so much that sometimes I can't quite believe that you aren't a mirage among the sheep and perhaps that wrong feeling may reflect itself in some letters. But I do truly know that you are the realest and most wonderful thing that ever happened.

This was one of the letters in which I sensed my mother may have reacted to something he had said, perhaps as far back as October, and he had to correct the impression in the next letter, perhaps in January. The strains of a relationship by letter are natural but, more than that, he was far away and often in extreme danger. This is also one of several letters in which he talks about being "down" or "a little depressed." At these points I sensed that he talked easily about getting "down," as if it were normal under the circumstances during a war, and I never felt he worried about it as a medical condition or a disturbing long-term mood.

Because Sullom Voe was in the middle of nowhere and close to enemy territory, the men were always on the lookout for enemy aircraft. They had even set up fake guns and armoured cars made of plywood to make the base look more protected than it was. On January 14, there was a surprise raid by a lone enemy bomber. I found the story, in Baker's 413 history, interesting because there was a humorous reference to my father, although not by name. That morning, the men had been told that a friendly Wellington bomber would be making some flights over the area. The medical officer (my father), on his way to Lerwick in the ambulance to get some supplies, spotted the Wellington overhead and waved merrily to what he thought was a friendly crew. The bomber turned out to be an enemy aircraft and dropped two 500-pound bombs, one exploding away from camp and the other hitting a Nissen hut where it surprised the occupant but didn't explode.

By now, from my research and reading the Baker history, I was realizing that my father was leaving much out of his letters: he couldn't tell the real stories because of the censorship. To compensate, he tried to recount one composite day in his life for the family back home. His father copied the long letter and circulated it among friends in Winnipeg in order to share his son's war experiences.

I first found one of the typed copies of the letter when I was a teenager. After my father's death, when she had to sell the house on Waverley, my mother had to get rid of most of the furniture from their large house in preparation for the move into her small quarters at South Drive. But she did manage to keep a few pieces that were important to her or to my father. One of these was a mahogany desk that had belonged to a seafaring relative of my great grandfather, R. T. Riley. The desk belonged to Captain Michael Riley and, probably because they had named their firstborn Michael, my parents inherited the desk. The drawers were huge, about eight inches deep and spanned the full width of the desk. In the third one, my mother kept family papers. There I discovered, one day when looking for wrapping paper, her diary in the thirteen scribblers and some of my father's letters from the war. I remember scanning the long letter describing a typical day, but not really being interested at the time—this was long before I knew anything about him. When I returned to it fifty-six years after my father's death, the copy of the letter had found a new home in my wooden box with the lift-up lid (my brother having inherited Captain Riley's desk). I sat in my study in Winnipeg one chilly fall morning and read the letter again. Suddenly, now that I was learning more about my parents' lives and my father's war experience, the letter became a wonderful gift in getting to know him. I laughed and cried as I imagined Bill Riley, my father, then twenty-five years old, huddled by his peat stove on the largest of the Shetland Islands trying to describe his days at war in a gentle and humorous way for a worried family back in Winnipeg.

Like a photograph gradually taking shape under developing solution, first the blacks and then the greys, the picture of Bill Riley began to appear. Fictionalizing his experience in the letter, my father seemed freer to reflect on his feelings as a doctor and was able to describe the things he cared about. His interest in psychiatry is apparent, as is his belief in treating the whole patient rather than just the physical wounds of war. I found many of his observations moving: his concern for the "sister back home" who was worrying about one of his patients, his comment that one of the boys, an artist, had "beautiful hands." He emerges as a loner, someone who doesn't hang around with the other officers but does his job solo and spends long hours in his room, reading and writing. I felt very close to the young man who was my dad as I read his letter from January 1942.

CHAPTER 8

AN EGG FOR BREAKFAST

SULLOM VOE, SHETLAND ISLANDS

JANUARY 25, 1942

Dear Mother and all my family,

I am going to try an experiment in writing tonight in order to give you some idea of how my days are spent. Life seems pretty routine and uneventful to me but perhaps if I try to describe a "specimen" day here it might be interesting to you and if I treat it in a general way I should be able to comply with censorship regulations. The following then is just any day—not one in particular.

I begin to exhibit signs of life about 0700 hours. My batman comes in, turns on the light, remarks that it is a miserable day and departs with shoes and tunic. I turn over and try hard to regain my unconscious state with incomplete success because it is cold and I can see my breath. The fire which I stoked up high last night has, of course, gone out. It nearly always does. I pull the covers over my head and try to remember what I was dreaming about. It's no use. I wish we had central heating. The batman re-enters with shoes and buttons shining and with a jug of hot water. He seems absurdly happy for this ungodly hour. He is cheerfully humming, about four notes flat "Home Sweet Home Again." He bangs the door as he departs. That last touch puts an end to the hope that I might be able to go back to sleep and stay there.

I suddenly remember that it was rumoured yesterday that there might be an egg for breakfast. I leap out of bed and grope for my toothbrush and squeeze some paste on it. I start brushing my teeth hard. Something is wrong—it tastes like shaving cream. It is shaving cream, a frantic grab for a glass of water and some furious gargling right this error. I am awake now anyway. I turn on the radio to get the morning news and start to shave. As soon as the news begins some unknown but undoubtedly bad type elsewhere in the camp turns on his electric razor. My radio emits a prolonged squawk and has to be turned off. My ablutions completed, I finish dressing, putting on each cold garment with a shudder. The exercise warms me up and I am hungry. I look at my watch. Only 3 minutes to make breakfast. Hurry, hurry, hurry. The mess is crowded with similar types to myself, who had heard something about eggs and are in just under the deadline. The egg rumour proves to be false but the breakfast is good anyway—porridge, sausage and mash, tea and toast. An after breakfast cigarette before the mess fire during which the squadron's probable activities for the day are discussed and the latest rumours about postings to sunnier climes are re-hashed. 0855 hours, and we all scatter to our respective places of activity or inactivity as the case may be.

Sick quarters has been a hive of activity for some time before I appear on the scene. Names and numbers of ailing airmen have been duly recorded in the appropriate books, temperatures and pulses have been taken, and everything is in readiness for the M.O.*'s daily ritual, morning sick parade. As I enter, the corridor is thronged with the sick in body or spirit or both. Most of them are attending for their morning dose of mist expectorans, the prerequisite for the treatment of all manner of ills in the* RAF.*, from acute laryngitis to the ubiquitous low back pain. A lesser number are waiting to be ushered through the portals of Medical Inspection Room for the first time. All who can manage to muster a cough or a sniffle do so as the* M.O. *passes*

by. A really grating cough is certain to draw at least a day's
E.D. (Excused Duty). The medical corporal is there with the
list as I sit down to my desk in the M.I. room. "Sergeant Plum!"
he bawls into the corridor. Plum enters. He is a pilot and has a
snuffly cold in his head. Nothing serious but he is put off flying
for 24 hours so that he will not run the risk of developing trouble
in his ears and sinuses under flying conditions. He will come up
three times today for some steam inhalations and some spray to
his nose.

"Corporal Galahad!" He is a fair-haired rosy cheeked youth
with a BBC accent. He was an artist in "civvy street." His
hands are beautiful. Here he disposes of unexploded time
bombs. His lower lip quivers almost imperceptively as he
apologetically blurts out his trouble. He has what we call in this
age of modern warfare "mechanized dandruff," in other words,
lice. He is very sensitive about it. I assure him that it occurs in
the best of families. I say that I have had them myself (this is
not true). Galahad seems relieved. The treatment is outlined
and arrangements are made to fumigate his clothing and
bedding. Also an inspection is planned for the other occupants
of his billet in case any should be harbouring fifth columnists.
Last on sick parade this morning is Flight Sergeant Prince. I
have kept Flight Prince to the last on purpose because I want to
spend some time with him. He has been complaining of
indigestion for some weeks now and it is interfering with his
efficiency as an air gunner. He is not sleeping at night. He is a
stocky well built kid from the South of England. He has the
physique of a young Goliath but his face is expressionless. No
light shines from his eyes. I ask him to sit down and hand him
a Canadian cigarette. He starts perceptively as I strike a match.
He accepts the proffered light with a hand that trembles a little
and that is deeply stained with nicotine. I nod to my corporal
who leaves the room. I don't know Prince very well. He spends
little time in the crew room and has never been in evidence at

any of the NCO's *parties that I have attended. His captain, I know, is not impressed with his abilities as an air gunner. He's considered a bit dumb. I ask him more about his complaints and we discuss them again for a few minutes in an unsatisfactory manner. I turn the conversation to operational flying. It doesn't seem to bother him particularly but he's not keen. He's not keen about anything. What was he doing before the war? Plumber's mate. Recreation? Football. His team were county champions. His shins were covered with scars. He never plays football now. Married? His face twists, he swallows and out it all comes in a torrent. Yes, Flight Sergeant Prince is married. His wife is 19, two years his junior. She is living, with their 8 month old baby, with her own people in Sussex. She is sick— she won't tell him in her letters what the matter is. He shows me a letter. None of the doctors are making her feel any better. She is taking three different kinds of medicine. Baby keeps her awake at night. They were married about a year ago, a couple of months after his father and mother and 4 brothers and sisters were killed when their house was blitzed. One sister wasn't hurt, at least not much. She is in a mental home now and young Prince hasn't seen her since the blitz. She writes to him though. He is not very happy about his sister. Fate has laid a heavy load on Flight Prince, broad though his shoulders are. The weight has numbed his senses somewhat. He doesn't realize he is carrying it. He only has indigestion and goes through life in a daze. One can't blot out the past or do much to alter the present but I will have to see a lot of Prince for the next while. I don't want him to go and live with his sister.*

Sick parade is over. An airman brings in a cup of tea. Airmen are always bringing tea at appropriate moments. Thank heaven there is no shortage of that. The station M.O. *comes in. He is a squadron leader and is in charge of the station which maintains the squadron. He is a very nice chap, not very senior in years to myself. He is a Cambridge blue. Tomorrow morning he will be duty* M.O. *and will conduct a similar rigmarole to the one just completed.*

It is after ten o'clock now and getting light outside. The blackouts are removed...

Ward rounds come next. Nobody is very sick this morning. LAC *Pimple's boil is ready for incision and we do that in the "crash room," one of us giving the anaesthetic and the other one wielding the knife. We usually alternate these two functions. Warrant officer Crabface is convalescing well from his pneumonia and will be ready for sick leave when we can arrange transport. Histories are written on the new admission and completed on a couple of discharges...*

It is noon by now and officers from station and squadron foregather in the mess. The mess proper consists of a large anteroom heated by four coal stoves, strategically placed so that no one part of the room may be warmer than any other part and the mean temperature can never exceed 60 degrees F. This is doubtless for reasons of health for it is a maxim in these parts that warm rooms are unhygienic. The anteroom is furnished with overstuffed leather chairs (field officers, for the use of) which are grouped about the stoves and with hard-backed chairs placed at intervals in the rest of the room for junior officers. It is considered bad form for a senior officer to sit in a junior officer's chair without first obtaining permission from the youngest P/O *present. The rule is infrequently broken. At one end of the anteroom is the bar. It is a real bar with a brass rail upon which feet may be rested. The mess prides itself on this rare possession. The bar is separated from the anteroom during working hours by a wooden shutter which may be lifted at stated times to permit normal commerce. When the shutter is closed, one can see on its surface a cartoon of a grim old lady which bears the words "As Lady Astor would say, 'Wait til the flap goes up.'" At noon there are usually quite a number of officers waiting and a good many more at 7 o'clock. The walls of the anteroom are tastefully adorned with pictures of the female form divine, creations of the well known George Petty. Under each picture is an appropriate caption such as "The light that lies in woman's eyes—and lies and lies and lies." These masterpieces strike close to the soul in such a bleak Empire post as ours.*

When the flap goes up a small number of those present converge like lightning on the space where the flap was. They want a quick one before lunch. A quick one usually consists of a half can of a fluid known as beer which tastes mostly like potato water to which has been added a small pinch of quinine. The word is not synonymous with a similar word "beer" widely employed in Canada.

At 12:30 lunch is served in the adjoining dining room. It is well furnished and meals are served at two long tables extending the length of the room. Members of the squadron usually sit together though there is no hard and fast seating rule. The station commander sits at the head of one of the tables and is usually surrounded by his own senior officers. Lunch today is a typically good substantial meal with no frills. Soup, bully beef with potatoes and the inevitable Brussels sprouts, a steamed pudding of sorts and coffee. The coffee is very poor but no worse than is found in any part of Britain. There are limitless supplies of bread and butter (the latter is margarine but one reaches the stage where the distinction may not be noticed and is certainly not commented upon). Table conversation is general and scrappy. "If I eat another Brussel sprout, I'll look like one." This remark not appreciated by the adjoining Englishmen. "What the hell do the government think they're doing?" This remark, as in every country in the world, generally concurred in.

Lunch over, the one o'clock news is turned on. It is one thing that doesn't change much with the days. Someone remarks:

"They ought to make a record of it." We sit around the mess for awhile, smoking, and then back to our respective offices. I have three men waiting for examination. They are ground men wanting to remuster as air crew. It probably isn't generally realized outside the Air Force that for every flying man there are ten, perhaps more, men on the ground to keep him flying. They are the fitters and riggers, the parachute packers, the marine craft section, the ground defence people, yes, and the accountants, the disciplinarians, the medical orderlies and a host of others. Their work isn't dangerous or glamorous under ordinary circumstances but it is very essential and often it is exceedingly dull and monotonous. The vast majority of them would give anything to be able to fly and have a chance to "really do something" but for reasons of health or age or education or special qualifications, a simple expediency, they are not allowed to. Without detracting from the air crew at all, these forgotten men should be remembered but few there are to sing their praises. The first airman this afternoon is, at present, a batman. When he enlisted he was ineligible for aircrew because of his deficient education. Since then, with the aid of the station education officer, he has spent his evenings working assiduously at algebra, geometry, trigonometry, and the mysteries of higher mathematics. The educational officer thinks he will do now, provided he can pass his physical examination. When he comes in, he is scared stiff. He has heard of this aircrew examination and he knows that M.O.'s are by nature tough and devoid of human understanding. His pulse is racing and his blood pressure is sky high. I proceed with the routine, talking the while, and gradually he contributes to the conversation. When we come to the reputedly difficult tests, I do them first. He thinks, "Good lord, if that man can do it, I certainly can." He does. At the end, his pulse and blood pressure are normal. "Did I pass, sir?" he falters. "Of course you did. Didn't you think you would?" "I didn't know, sir." Amazement written all over his face.

The second man is easy. He looks on the examination as just another one of those things. He's alright.

The third man is out from the word go. He is colour blind and quite ineligible for the air job he aspires to. He can't understand it. He didn't know he was colour blind and he doesn't believe it. He wants to see a specialist. I am sorry and quite agreeable to the specialist idea. He leaves in a disgruntled frame of mind.

• • •

After looking in the ward, I wander across to the Flying Rations Store. It is snowing and there is quite a wind blowing. I hope we have no aircraft still out. The Flying Rations store, which I more or less unofficially supervise, is designed to provide good food for crews out on long sorties. Mostly it is a matter of trying to make bricks without straw but all in all we don't do too badly. Everything seems in order here. I sign a hopeful indent for some oranges and eggs and then drop into the Crew Room. This is a comfortable enough hut used as a gathering place for aircrew when on the ground. It is fitted up much as a sitting room with magazines strewn about and a little radio going. In a corner, a group of NCO's are playing stud poker with halfpennies, a practice I might say, strictly at variance with Air Force law. A sergeant Observer invites me (if I have any money) to join in. I decline, more on account of the time of day than on principle. Some concern is expressed by those present about our aircraft K (for Katie) which set out on a patrol early this morning. If this weather continues she won't be able to come back here but there are lots of other stations in Britain to which she could be diverted.

I drift back to the mess and have tea. It is a regular sit-down meal with bread and butter and, this afternoon, jam. Somebody has had a jar from home. The Flight Commander is a bit concerned about K for Katie. The weather is bad all over the British Isles and is not improving. I go to my hut to prepare for a bath. There is a regular Western Canadian blizzard blowing. The wind speed must be 40 to 50 mph. It is quite dark now because it is after 1800 hours. I have just begun to undress when a service police airman comes in. "They are going to lay a flare-path for K for Katie. Are you going out, sir?" Of course I am, but I can't understand what they are thinking of, trying to bring an aircraft in here tonight. I gird myself with sweaters, flying boots, heavy gloves, a scarf and cover all with a waterproof Macintosh. Armed with a torch I go to the operations room. The Squadron C.O. and the Flight Commander are there and look worried. The weather has closed in everywhere and K for Katie will have to land here. She only has petrol for another six hours and won't be able to stay up until the storm blows over. She is due back in about an hour. My ambulance is waiting outside and the duty pilot and I ride down to the pier in it. The duty pilot is a Canadian from Vancouver and is normally captain of our F for Freddie. Tonight his job is to lay the lighted floats in the bay so that Peters, the Captain of K for Katie, can see where to come in. In weather like this, it is a desperately important task. We cruise out into the bay in the pinnace towing the flares behind us. The coxswain remarks that it is a bloody awful night. Hank, the duty pilot, replies in unprintable agreement. The snow is driving down furiously and at times we can scarcely see six feet ahead. The wind is blowing in intermittent squalls and our little craft is tossed about like a cork in the heavy sea. It seems like suicide to consider landing an aircraft now but he will have to get down some way. Perhaps the gale will subside but it appears to be getting worse every minute. Finally the flare floats are anchored one by one, to mark the safe approach. How the right spot was located I don't know. I can't see anything but the row of bobbing lights behind us. Now there is nothing to do but wait. I glance across the tiny cabin at my orderly who is being noisily seasick in the corner. I check over my first aid supplies. They might be needed tonight. Hank and I talk about nothing in particular. We don't mention what we are both thinking as the hours slip by. I must have dozed off and I sit up with a start. The watch on deck thinks he hears an engine. We go up. The weather is still pitiless but if that is K she has to land. Better a bad landing here than miles from help or a crack up on those bleak hills around us. It's K for Katie all right. She is circling over us. She must be nearly at the end of her endurance. The Teutonic gods of Wagner must be controlling the elements tonight. The gale is at its height. Katie is approaching to land. We can see her landing lights and the spew of her exhausts. Good God, the end flare has overturned! She's coming in anyway. She's going to overshoot. She's cut her engines. "Get that searchlight on the aircraft!" They've smashed up. No, by heaven, she's waterborne and safe. "Get a towline on to her quick, she'll never taxi in." We drop a lifebelt with a rope attached and the aircraft manages to pick it up, just in time. She was being blown perilously close to the rocky shore. We begin to tow her in. Lord, what a night. Thank God they're safe. What the devil is that? The aircraft is firing rockets. They're in trouble. We have a little dinghy alongside and it is slid back along the tow-rope to the aircraft. The crew is brought off. K for Katie is sinking. The seas were too heavy for her. Well the crew is safe anyway and a weary and bedraggled lot they are. They can scarcely believe they are here. They all crowd into the cabin. A young Sergeant Observer is violently sick and has been all through the storm. They are all soaked and shivering. I disperse generous tots of rum. It is too rough to make tea. Half of them are asleep as they stand within a couple of minutes. We have to spend the rest of the night on board the pinnace. We can't go alongside the pier until the storm subsides. Nobody talks. They are past that. We have a hard job waking them when dawn breaks and we go ashore.

It's ten o'clock in the morning again now and we have breakfast. Then bed and what a great place that is today. I pull the cover over me and relax. Ho hum. That's another day gone anyway.

The above may give you some idea of the kind of life I lead. It is a composite picture but it is all based on experience and it might have conceivably occurred in one day. Sometimes things seem a bit dull but they really aren't and all in all I think it is a fairly worthwhile way to spend a year or so. It looks as if I am in for a bit of a change now and if it is as interesting as my past 20 months I shall have no cause for complaint.

Your affectionate son, Bill.

CHAPTER 9

AT SEA AGAIN

In early 1942, the members of Squadron 413 got word that they were being moved, probably welcome news given the conditions in the Shetlands. The men were given leave before departing by sea for their next posting, and Bill spent his in London.

In February, 1942, he thanked his parents for care packages.

> *Dear Mother and Dad,*
>
> *I'm in the Park Lane Hotel in London, on leave…I only got letters from you numbered 2 and 5 since Christmas, many have gone astray, the boats can't carry enough to the isolated location. However, just before I left I received in one day 3,000 cigarettes (including some from the Scotts, God bless 'em), your much belated and excellent windbreaker and bags of assorted and welcome food.*

On his last night in London, Bill again visited his family's old friend Duffin. The next morning, he wrote to his parents:

> *This is the last letter you will have from me for a very long time and, though it won't tell you very much, I know you will understand that is absolutely necessary.*

He described his last night in London. He and Duffin went to a show, had dinner and talked in his hotel room for hours.

> *He surely filled in the parental gap that night and I think we both felt very close to you all. He is a great person and has done more for me than I can say.*

When this opportunity broke, I wired HQ to cancel my previous request which had already been approved. My logical reasoning is hard to articulate but, at the risk of sounding sentimental, the combination of Riley and Collum that is me couldn't have done otherwise. I think you will both agree, when you know the circumstances. Anyway, it promises to be a new and interesting chapter. Again I am in the vanguard of the RCAF Medical Services and again, with no regrets, I have thrown away the chances for an early promotion.

Bill said he could talk very little about personal plans but added that he had chosen his next move. He had also, he said, abandoned the chance of coming home anytime soon. He now measured the time remaining away in years rather than months—again with no regrets.

As I read my father's letter, I wondered what my mother, in her "waiting life," would have thought of this decision. My father had a deep sense of duty and an idealistic view of war and what it could accomplish. He had been brought up in the Riley family to value war service and to admire the two uncles he was named for, but the horrors of World War I and the wholesale slaughter of Canadian men were not yet common knowledge. He really believed what senior officers were telling him about the opportunity ahead. Earle Duffin, who had experienced the first war, may have been more realistic about the challenges ahead.

In March, 1942, Duffin wrote to his old friend Herb Riley in Winnipeg of the meeting with his son Bill as he left for the new posting.

As the evening progressed, it became evident to me that, as it was near enough his last evening, he wanted to spend it with somebody who had known his father and mother for many years, and as both his Uncle Harold and Uncle Bill and myself had similar sort of leaves in London during the last war, it was interesting for the older and the younger generation to be going through similar experiences and discussing together problems that would lie ahead. I appreciated it because he is a great lad and full of pep and courage and is certainly taking a very long journey.

My father and the rest of the ground crew of 413 Squadron left by ship from Liverpool March 17, 1942.

My father's letters from At Sea revealed little of the larger picture. The men on board didn't know much about what was going on in the war and were not even sure of their destination. His letters did express the boredom of a long sea voyage with nothing to do but think and reflect. By April, Bill had been At Sea a month and had had much time to speculate about the future. Although war speculation was important, thoughts inevitably turned to what these events meant personally.

On April 18, 1942, he wrote his family from At Sea again, reinforcing his belief that war was necessary but showing some anxiety about what would happen when it was over.

> We need strong leaders now but we will need them equally when the war is over and the need may not be so obvious. The most important thing is that _we_ must have the choosing of them and that I suppose is the real war aim of most of us. The Germans and the Japs would give us leaders alright but not the ones we want…from the personal standpoint it seems futile to speculate on post-war possibilities until the end is in sight. I would like to spend at least a year and if possible more on post graduate work as there will be a glut of medicos with qualifications as mediocre as my own. However, circumstances alone can decide that.

On April 29, 1942, he wrote what sounded to me like a melancholy birthday note from At Sea to his parents.

> Of all my birthdays this is undoubtedly the least eventful, being so completely out of touch with everyone who has been any sort of influence in my life in the last 26 years. Perhaps the next one will see the old ties renewed. There seems little point in celebrating this one."

And on May 11, 1942, another from At Sea, to Aunty Anne. The journey was feeling long and boring and, instead of being able to talk about what was really happening on the voyage, he speculated about the progress of the war, admitting that he was "padding" the letter.

My Dear AMC,

...It's cool today as there is a great wind blowing across the ocean and it is heaven to be able to sit without perspiration dripping from every pore. The journey has seemed endless but it can't go on for much longer and we shall all be delighted to set foot on dry land once again...The fragments of news that we receive are few and far between and I am most curious to know what happened in the Canadian conscription plebiscite. All we have heard is that the troops voted overwhelmingly to release the government from its pledge and, because that is all we have heard, I can't help being a little suspicious that the country may have turned it down. I do sincerely hope not because it seems suicide to blindly tie the hands of a government that is supposed to be making war...

The war seems to be progressing without any startling developments in any direction. I'm glad that we took the initiative in Madagascar which looks to be pretty well in our hands. The much vaunted German offensive on the Eastern front has not yet started and it looks as if it will be fiercely resisted if not entirely stemmed. The Jap navy is still a question mark and if it can be seriously damaged without too great a loss to ourselves, the advantage should be most important. As I am writing, there is a naval battle in the Coral Sea but the reports are conflicting. It is never wise to attempt to prophesy but, at a risk, I would say that the Russians will keep the Germans occupied in Europe this summer and that the United Nations will do much to regain their wallop in the Far East, leaving next year clear for an effective offensive. I don't think we shall lose Ceylon—I certainly hope not, and I believe Australia will remain intact though the battle may be quite considerable. The Near East and Gibraltar and Malta are posers and I should think a lot depends on Dorlan and French West Africa. Anyway, I think we will have them on ice in 1944 at least. By the time you read this it will probably look pretty silly. However, that is the way it looks to me just now.

For myself I have little news. I am well and cheerful—if not happy, I am at least thoroughly complacent. There are a few things about my present and future environment that I do not relish particularly but I much prefer to be here than in England or, under the circumstances, at home. And perhaps I may be able to do something to correct the evils which I dislike....Sorry to write such a "padded" letter.

My love, your affectionate Bill

When my father offered this speculation to his aunt from what he could make of media reports, pilots from his own 413 squadron had, just the week before, saved Ceylon from a dramatic attack by the Japanese. It appears he did not know anything of the Easter raid.

1.

RCAF *Squadron 413*

2.

3.

"His hat was always bigger than his head," or Bill Riley, 1940

Dr. Riley, 413 Medical Officer, Ceylon, 1943

4.

With friends in Ceylon, 1943

5.

*My Dad (hands in pockets)
interviewed by the BBC in the
Shetlands, 1941*

6.

Wedding day in Winnipeg, March, 1944

7.

Honeymoon 1944, New York

8.

Mike and I in the dining room, 749 South Drive, Fort Garry

9.

Family Portrait taken just before my father died

10.

I visit Gordon Ireland, Vancouver Island, 2003

CHAPTER 10

THE FAR EAST

When the men in Squadron 413 left the cold, dark north Atlantic and the barren landscape of the Shetlands and headed for a tropical paradise in Ceylon, my father didn't really know why. His letter to his parents indicated that he felt he had some choice in the move. He was probably told he was headed to the Far East and the move was likely described as a good medical experience, a chance to learn about tropical disease. And he knew that the closest enemy for a time was to be Japan and not Germany.

As I read my father's letters, I tried to fill the gaps with some reading about World War II. I learned that, when Squadron 413 left for the Far East in early 1942, the war was going badly for the Allies. By April, as Bill's convoy ship headed for India, British Prime Minister Winston Churchill had a string of defeats to explain to Parliament and he was facing a vote of non-confidence. President Roosevelt's fireside chat in February tried to boost Allied morale but the Americans were losing the war in the Pacific. By January, the Japanese had captured Hong Kong in eighteen days, Manila in twenty-six and Singapore in seventy. Only by the end of 1942 would the Allies' fortunes begin to turn around gradually. The successful defence of Ceylon in April of that year was a key turning point for the British forces and for Churchill. He later called it "the most dangerous moment" of the war.

As I searched for something in my father's war service that might give me a clue to the circumstance leading up to his suicide, I remembered that he had been mentioned in dispatches, a list of servicemen credited with meritorious service. I wondered whether the award was for some particularly dangerous or heroic act. I was still looking for something that offered a clue to his death. Perhaps there was a buddy that he thought he should have been able to save or a battle that could have resulted in flashbacks later. Although his letters from the North Atlantic made reference to some action, the most dramatic public event connected with his service seemed to be the Japanese attack on Ceylon in April of 1942.

The newspaper clippings in my mother's scrapbook called that attack "the Easter raid." Squadron 413 was credited with saving Colombo, the capital of Ceylon. The photograph of the officers aboard ship, including H. W. Riley, medical officer of the squadron, ran in the Winnipeg papers under the headline "The Men Who Saved Colombo." Sheila saved the clippings. Starved for news of their loved ones overseas, the families at home must have read these stories hungrily.

However, as I read them more than fifty years later, something was not making sense. How could my father be one of the men who saved Colombo when his letters clearly showed that he was still At Sea when the Easter raid took place? I began to read more about the attack on Ceylon. I discovered that a lot had been written about the moment when the Japanese almost took Ceylon, including a book called *The Most Dangerous Moment*. (Michael Tomlinson, Granada Publishing Limited, 1979, now out of print).

A victory in Ceylon would have given Japan entrance to the British Empire from the Far East and control of the Indian Ocean, an important supply line. The tiny British colony off the southeast coast of India was a tropical island with an abundance of tea plantations but almost no military protection at the time. Because there was not even a proper airstrip, it was particularly vulnerable. By early March, Japanese fleet movements in the Indian Ocean were detected and an attack was feared. It was part of the long-range Japanese plan to take over the Indian Ocean.

By May, American cryptographers in MAGIC (like the British code cracking organization ULTRA) had collected good information that the Japanese fleet, the same one that had attacked Pearl Harbor in December 1941, was in the area. The British scrambled to pull together a defence in Ceylon. Naval units and maritime air squadrons were quickly summoned and long-range aircraft were needed to scout the ocean for the attackers. The flat-bellied Cats that had been stationed in the Shetlands were perfect for the job.

The flight crews from 413 left the Shetlands in March by air in their "flying boats." The first 413 Catalina, flown by Leonard Birchall, a young Canadian pilot originally from St. Catherines, Ontario, arrived in Ceylon on April 2. He joined others from 413 who had set up camp in Koggala at the southern tip of the island, surrounded by coconut plantations.

The Cats, as they arrived from the Shetlands, were immediately sent on nightly patrols to look for signs of the Japanese fleet. On April 4, out on their first survey flight, Birchall and his crew could not believe their eyes. At first it was just a tiny speck but it soon became clear they had spotted the Japanese fleet in the distance, 350 miles south of Ceylon. The crew radioed a report back to the base and, according to the newspaper clippings I was reading in my mother's scrapbook, Birchall's Catalina was never heard from again. The plane was shot down and Birchall was presumed dead, lost at sea along with his crew. The protocol was to send a message three times to verify the contents. Birchall and his crew had managed to send the frantic warning only twice before the radio went dead.

By midnight, the Japanese fleet was 270 miles away and, warned by Birchall's message, the base in Colombo readied for attack. They were able to hide most of the British naval fleet and defend the island successfully, preventing Japanese troops from gaining an important strategic foothold. In June, the Canadian Air Minister reported to Parliament that seven Canadian airmen had destroyed eight Japanese bombers and one fighter in the Easter raid on Colombo.

The newspapers the Riley family at home was reading reported that 440 members of Squadron 413 were settled in a palm-fringed coastal base on the island and were sending flights out day and night in search of further Japanese attackers. One of the men reported that he was still in shock, having moved in a matter of months from "one of the coldest, most barren spots on earth" to the tropics.

A combination of British propaganda and misleading information meant the news families at home received about the Easter raid was incomplete. The British had barely managed to hold the island and losses were heavy. Military historians are sure that if the Japanese had attacked again, they would have been successful. Luckily, the Japanese turned to other things. But the British news releases about the period were positive. Although some twenty-three ships were sunk by the Japanese off the coast of India, the losses were not made public. When the attack on Colombo was announced, the Allies claimed heavy enemy losses. What was really a British embarrassment was claimed as a victory. And, as I pieced together the story over fifty years later, I realized my father was still At Sea, nowhere near the action.

As I read my father's letters from Ceylon, I was still looking for any clue to his suicide, any serious trauma that might tell me something more about his death. I began to find out what I could about the war in the Far East. I learned that, after the Easter Raid, Britain built up an offensive in Ceylon but the island was never attacked again.

• • •

One day, on my lunch hour, as I was browsing through books for sale at tables in a shopping mall, I picked up a true story written by a woman who had helped Canadians escape to France from Germany during the war. A cheerful veteran in uniform complete with medals presiding over the table recommended the book. We began chatting. I told him I was interested in the war because my father had been in the air force.

"What squadron?" he asked.

"413," I responded.

"Oh," he said, "that's a very famous squadron because of the Saviour of Ceylon."

I mentioned the newspaper clippings in my mother's scrapbook about the Japanese raid on Ceylon. I said I knew the dramatic story about Birchall, the young Canadian who had died warning the British of the attack. He studied me carefully as I talked and hesitated a moment before he spoke.

"You know, of course, that Leonard Birchall is alive."

Suddenly, the heavy curtain on the past fell away. I felt a physical lightening inside. That moment was the beginning of finding the real story of my father at war and the Easter Raid. It was the breakthrough I needed in my search for people who knew my father during the war.

Finding a hero from my father's wartime service was like discovering ghosts from the past. My most frequent, recurring fantasy about my father was that everyone had lied and he was secretly still alive. One day I would find him. The ghost of Leonard Birchall was a beginning, a historical figure from the past coming alive. If he could be alive, so could my father. He would help me find him.

Reading my father's letters, I had been imagining those young men stationed in the Shetland Islands, travelling by ship for months around the Cape of Good Hope until they reached the tropical island off the eastern tip of India, only to find that one of their squadron's own pilots had died, shot down spotting the Japanese just off the coast. Now I was finding out that the pilot hero had survived the war. It was like finding a part of my father.

"Birchall and his men were taken prisoner and spent the rest of the war in a Japanese prisoner of war camp. And Birchall is in his eighties but very much alive. I saw him when he came to Winnipeg last year," my new friend in the shopping mall told me. He said it was quite possible that Birchall knew my father because he had served in the Shetlands and then had flown his Cat to Ceylon. He didn't have his address but promised to help me find him. When I told my brother Mike about Leonard Birchall, he said simply, "We wouldn't exist if it weren't for him." I had never thought of it that way but, presumably, if the British had not been warned by Birchall and the Japanese had taken Ceylon, the ship carrying the ground crew from the Shetlands would have been captured or perhaps sunk at sea and my father would never have come home.

I continued my search and, after weeks of phone calls, found Leonard Birchall, by then Air Commodore Birchall and living in Kingston. Over the phone, he said he did not know my father, having spent a very short time in the Shetlands. But, in the midst of a busy life travelling and giving speeches, he took the time to dig up the names of four Squadron 413 veterans who had been in Ceylon at the same time as my father. He sent me names and addresses by letter and I quickly wrote to all of them, knowing that time was important.

One June evening, the phone rang and I listened to a voice leave a message.

"I am calling from Courtney, B.C. and I knew your father during the war. "

I rushed to pick up the phone. Gordon Ireland had been 18 when he enlisted and so he was then only 80, a relatively young veteran.

"I remember your Dad vividly. He must have been about twenty-five at the time but he was slight and his hat always looked bigger than his head. He was our medical officer."

The ghosts were surfacing. For the first time, I found myself talking to someone who had known my father during those war years no one had ever talked to me about. They were the lost years everyone blamed for his death but no one really knew anything about them. Now those years came alive for me as I listened to a complete stranger on Vancouver Island talk about the father I had never known.

And there was none of the anxious holding back or the cautious concern for my feelings. Gordon Ireland seemed to know that I would want stories, that I was hungry for any memories he had. We talked for a short time that night and he later recounted what he remembered in a letter.

> For the short time I was acquainted with your dad, I remember him as being a young man for such an important position, serving close to 300 men in a Far East tropical situation.

He then supplied a very different picture of what was happening to my father in April of 1942 than the one I had from the letters. I had my father's own description of the never-ending sea voyage, the enervating boredom and the excitement of a short stop in Bombay. I also had the mysterious newspaper article reporting that my father and the rest of 413 squadron had saved Ceylon from the Japanese attack.

The other thing I will always remember about your father, as will all those travelling on our troop ship, the Nieuw Holland, a converted cargo ship from March 17, 1942 (departed Liverpool) to June 1, 1942 (arrived Colombo), was the mutiny.

The men (331 ground crew including nine officers) rebelled against the unsanitary, crowded conditions aboard, the rotten, stinking food and lack of fresh water. The men were cranky and restless and fights broke out as they demanded shore leave. They broke into the kitchen and threw the rotten fish overboard.

A meeting was called when we pulled into Bombay. The authorities were calling for some serious action against the mutineers, which were many, when your dad, as senior medical officer on board, called the mutiny justifiable. He authorized shore leave for health reasons and called for the ship to bring in provisions suitable for our health and well-being. Our problem prior to this remedial action was that the eggs were rotten, the water contaminated, the fish wormy and bread full of weevils. I weighed 135 pounds when I got on board and 113 when I got off. Your father's actions, given his rank and the fact that he was taking on much senior rank—a British Army Colonel and the ship's Captain—took a lot of guts. But he made his point. They seemed to understand that, if they did not take heed, he would hold them responsible.

It was stories like this that began to make me feel proud of my father. It was a new feeling for me. I had always felt a sense of shame for what he had done, to my mother, to his parents and to us. But that was disappearing.

Bill's letters did not mention the mutiny although he did talk about the excitement of finally enjoying shore leave in Bombay. Then the men were back on the ship for the short journey to Ceylon. In May, just after the Bombay stop, he wrote from At Sea to his sister Eleanor. The letter was full of fun and a sense of adventure.

Well I am on my way again but not for long this time. I gather we are going to a pretty lonely jungly spot but that should be teeming with interest for me. It's a great life and the wanderlust in me gets stronger every day...

Finally they were getting close to their destination. On May 23, 1942, he wrote his parents again from At Sea, sounding positive about the posting now that he was almost there:

The journey is nearly over and, though it has not been too bad, the latter part has been tedious enough and I shall be grateful to have a spot of my own where I can unpack my belongings, even if it is only a tent in the jungle...My brief stay in India was most enjoyable and made me feel I wouldn't have missed this experience for anything in the world...I've heard that others had applied for this job...it will be a unique medical experience that years of post-graduate work would be unlikely to give me.

I do feel now that I would like to spend a long time in these parts and that is good because, in all probability, I shall! I like the people, the food, the customs, in fact everything except the arrogant British attitude that is appalling.

This was one of my father's remarks that, combined with Gordon Ireland's story of confronting British officers during the mutiny, told me he found the British colonial attitude tiresome. The feeling was to grow during his time in India. He read E. M. Forester's *Passage to India* and recommended it to his father back home but cautioned that it was almost like reading banned literature in the colonies.

As I followed my father's journey to Ceylon, I thought about how it would feel to be a pawn in a chess game played by politicians and military leaders whose decisions could easily be the result of personal ambition or ignorance. I marvelled at men like my father who trusted their lives to the military machine. I also thought about how easily my generation of post-world War II "babyboomers" was able to dismiss war as wrong during the heady activist days of the late 1960s when we were coming of age during the Viet Nam War. I realized it wasn't so simple to promote 'peace not war' for young people like my father who believed peace could only be won by stopping an aggressor like Hitler. I found it hard to fault the sacrifice in their personal lives these Canadians were prepared to make for future generations like mine.

Bill's first letter home from Ceylon, dated June 12, 1942, said he hadn't heard from his family since February, almost four months with no word from home. Not only had he endured a grueling sea voyage but he had no letters to connect him with family.

On June 24, 1942, he wrote:

> I attended a devil dance in a Buddhist Temple the other day, which was quite an experience. The Sinhalese are interesting and friendly people. As I write they are beating their drums in the jungle behind us.

And, in July:

> I am living with eight other officers in a sprawling palm-leaf bungalow that is surprisingly waterproof. We are situated on the edge of the jungle.

> ...My job keeps me very busy these days and the medical and public health experience is tremendous. I am at present looking after a pretty large unit alone and am many miles from any assistance. I am glad that that is so as the glamour of the Orient is wearing off and I should be pretty tired of life otherwise.

Other accounts of squadron life (Baker's history, *The Most Dangerous Moment* and *Wings of the Dawning, The Battle for the Indian Ocean, 1939-45* by Arthur Banks, 1996, Images Publishing [Malvern] Ltd.) also mention monotonous days of debilitating humid heat and nights under mosquito netting without a breeze. In August of that first summer, a 413 aircraft had an accident in training and the flight engineer was killed and several crew members injured. The Japanese sunk a British ship and the Royal Navy rescued the survivors.

Since my father could write of none of this, he wrote his mother September 1, 1942, from Ceylon.

Dear Mother and all of you,

I have no writable news about myself. Days are very routine and my responsibilities with the squadron are really of a very junior quality compared to some of the jobs I have had to do. I will be very glad if a change comes my way but, except by wishful thinking, I can see no sign of it. I've been with it a year now! The monsoon has dropped and the dry season set in with a steady oppressive heat which, though not really excessive, is a bit enervating....

Often he worried about the effects of his letters on his mother and wrote the next month to apologize:

Dear Mother...

I think when I last wrote I may have sounded a bit on the glum side and I want to correct that impression tonight...all in all I am most happy albeit quite ready for any change that might present itself, as is usual when my evanescent self has stayed put for any length of time.

On November 14, 1942, he was preparing for another Christmas away.

I hope to write an interesting letter soon...Merry Christmas and a Happy New Year...

A letter written December 30, 1942, from Ceylon, praising the Red Cross, gives some idea of the primitive hospital conditions he was working with:

To My dear family...

At this point I must pass on a word of appreciation to you for the Canadian Red Cross. I have obtained from them for our rather primitive little hospital here dressing gowns, pajamas, bed jackets and bandages and a great selection of delicacies such as calves-foot jelly, jam, etc.. Their gifts are great and all I need to do is ask and they send...I had some sheets from them. They were particularly useful as it sometimes takes as long as two months to have laundry done and back here and for some time

> *we couldn't even provide dirty sheets on our hospital beds.... their comfort kits for stranded injured picked up in the sea or elsewhere are quite ideal...*

And then he described his Christmas.

> *On Christmas Eve the Sergeant pilots invited me down to their mess and for once the beer was plentiful and we had a grand sing song evening, people from different parts of the world regaling the others with songs or stories peculiar to themselves. On Christmas morning we got some beer and fed it to our patients and then went to the officers' mess where we were hosts to the sergeants. Then the officers and sergeants proceeded to the airmens' mess where we put on chefs' caps and served them with their Christmas dinner. We had the band and plum pudding and even a small slice of turkey for everyone...the only bad part was that our over-zealous hosts kept surreptitiously slipping tots of assorted low grade gin, rum or whiskey into our beer and we never quite knew where we were. However we all had a glorious time. Need I say that the following day was one of the worst I have ever experienced and I was the only one in the squadron who couldn't report on sick parade...everyday I am having new and interesting experiences and meeting new people and liking life...I thought Churchill's speech to congress was his best yet. He certainly is a super man...I do hope they get this Jap situation in hand or I will be annoyed about being over here. However, Germany is our real enemy even if Japan is closer.*

In early January, my father wrote his parents that the squadron was excited by the award of a DSO to the squadron's new commanding officer, Scotty (J. C. Scott). He couldn't say what the award was for but added that another Winnipegger, Gordon Bracken, had been involved and he didn't know of any other "flying boat" DSO's anywhere. He said that he was doubly censored from Ceylon and couldn't say anything more.

I found out that the flight that won Commander Scott the DSO was one of the few offensive raids 413 undertook from Ceylon. The bombing raid, which gathered valuable enemy information over Sumatra, was one of the longest on record, covering over two thousand miles in all and lasting more than seventeen hours. Despite the occasional excitement for the pilots, my father was finding his days as a medical officer long and boring.

On January 13, 1943, he wrote to Dr. Fred Cadham at the Provincial Laboratory in Winnipeg. My grandfather was sent a copy of the letter and had it typed out to circulate to friends and family as some news of his son. I found it interesting because, as it was to a fellow medical doctor in infectious diseases, Bill was specific about the diseases he was encountering. Both malaria and dengue had been mentioned to me as illnesses that my father might have had while in the tropics.

> *Your air letter-card, dated Dec. 8 arrived today and it was a thrill to hear from you…My sojourn in the tropics is adding a chapter to my life that will be a memorable one and I trust will be an asset in the days to come…From the medical standpoint we see much of interest clinically, though the unit M.O. is always a bit frustrated by not being able to follow up his more intriguing cases, which are transferred to general hospitals some distance away. Fortunately, we have very little malaria, though it is of course the number one possibility. We have a lot of dengue, which we treat in our sick quarters, and the occasional dysentery, both bacillary and amoebic, which of course we have to transfer to centres where laboratory procedures are available. The most time-consuming part of our job is directing the destruction of flies and mosquitoes, watching the water supply and sewage disposal and attempting to convert the stubborn infidels, both in and out of the service, who stoutly maintain that if you get a disease it is predestined anyway and that this pogrom on insect vectors is just another of the doc's fads.*

> *For the rest, Ceylon is a delightful paradise, but awfully far from home. It's a fine thing to walk along a palm-silhouetted beach in the tropical moonlight with the tinkle of the Buddhist temple bells punctuating the undulating swell of the warm*

breakers, the distant staccato accompaniment of a lone native drummer in the background and the atmosphere heavy with the exotic scents of the lush verdure; but at this point I'll trade it for the corner of Portage and Main in a January blizzard.

As I read the letters from Ceylon, I pictured my father spending his days in the poorly equipped little hospital, occasionally treating injured airmen rescued at sea but mostly doing routine physicals. He was sounding bored with the medicine and tired of the life. Although I was getting no closer to any explanation of his suicide, I was getting to know my father: reading his letters was like having the conversation I never had with him.

From his letters I got the impression that Ceylon was a relatively quiet place to be spending the war years. But now I had another perspective from one of the squadron members who was there at the same time. Gordon Ireland wrote from his home in Courtney, British Columbia and this time he included snapshots from 1942 that brought the place to life for me. He also told me about the time he had been one of my father's patients.

It is difficult to know where to start after so many years. As squadron M.O., a F/Lt at the time, your dad was assisted by three medical orderlies…

Of importance to me was that I suffered from foot rot from my small toe to the next two toes, which developed from the beach strong undertow and the sand cutting them up, then infection and, in the Tropics, infection runs rampant. Subsequently, the three toes appeared to be hanging by a thread and should have come off but with your dad's persistence and good treatment, they were finally saved.

I share the pictures with you as I have no further use of them. They will show you what your dad was exposed to while in Ceylon, places he would have seen when not occupied with his medical duties. On our base, if one were very sick, they would ship us to Colombo to the British medical hospital. If one's sickness was mild, you would get excused duty for 48 to 72 hours for diagnosis spent overnight in the base clinic. Malaria, dengue fever and V.D. were the norms along with dysentery and jaundice. As you can imagine, he was kept very busy.

As I flipped through the photos Gordon Ireland sent, images formed. He had written short notes on the back of each.

A convoy ship belched black smoke as rickshaws lined up waiting for passengers. *This was the scene greeting us in Colombo. We got straight on a train to Camp Boosa.*

A cart piled high with what looks like a straw covering is escorted by men in white suits, one walking and one on a bicycle, and followed by a truck marked 'Daily News Service'. *A street scene in the nearest town to our base, Galle.*

A beautiful woman in a long formal gown draped with a sash across one shoulder holds a child in a puffy white dress, sandals and a lace hair band. *This is Alice the lace lady and her daughter. Her husband was a gem merchant and lost at Singapore. Your Dad would, as many of us did, have purchased some of her beautiful lace work.* I never saw lace from Ceylon but my mother left me a necklace and bracelet my father had given her when he returned. With them is a signed certificate which guarantees they hold genuine stones from a gem merchant in Ceylon.

Sinhalese boys hold a huge lobster by its long feelers with the beach and breakers in the background. *A day's catch on the Beach we frequented daily. Your dad would place it "out of bounds" during the monsoon weather. However we would only be charged for violation if we got in trouble and required rescuing.*

Two young boys at the base of a coconut tree, which they had obviously climbed, hold the fruit they had gathered. *The juice is cloudy and a very good tonic and pleasant to drink.*

Other pictures show women weaving copra to build the servicemen huts at Koggala and RCAF men with local people who served as room boys and laundry women. Gordon Ireland explained that only one serviceman from Quebec had a camera and he used to take pictures and then sell them to the others. It turned out my father and Gordon had paid him for some of the same pictures.

A postcard displays the huge Galle Face Hotel in Colombo with striped awnings and palm trees in front. *Your Dad would have been here on more than one occasion. It was for officers only.*

Another of The Resthouse in Negombo. *This was not far from our base. The meals were always good and inexpensive.*

And the corner of Nuwara Eliya Lake, a tranquil scene with mist lifting off the lake. *He would have been here for sure to get some relief from the heat down south.*

Gordon Ireland also described what must have been a too-frequent task in the squadron, writing letters of condolence to the families back home. He remembered particularly the one to Leonard Birchall's wife in Canada. The squadron leader drafted a letter of condolence to Mrs. Birchall, stating the squadron's admiration at the bravery and sorrow at the loss. Ireland remembers a moment of pride when, as the squadron's youngest member (20 by then), he gave up his RCAF colors Hat Flash, worn inside his pith helmet band, to enclose in the letter as a memento.

News that Birchall had survived was received in the U.S. sometime during the war, written by a U.S. Navy POW in a card to his sister back home. But the men in 413 did not know Birchall was alive until after the war was over. My father may never have known.

• • •

During the time I was exploring the possible interpretations of my father's autopsy report, I made another connection with someone who had spent some years in Ceylon during the war. I had called Manitoba's chief medical examiner, to help with the autopsy findings. As it turned out, he was particularly interested in my story because he was from Sri Lanka (formerly Ceylon). I sat in his office while he made phone calls trying to find hospital records from 1947. Relying on the autopsy's report of the needle mark on the inside of my father's elbow, his theory was that my father had had a blood test shortly before he died. He thought there might be some surviving record and he used his authority to try to find one. No luck. The records did not go back that far.

But, as we talked, he remembered that he had met a Winnipeg doctor who spent some of the war in Ceylon. He called him and we arranged to meet.

Dr. Maurice Shnider was a navigator in WWII with the RCAF and was stationed in Ceylon in 1943, just after my father left. Although they didn't know each other, he was able to tell me that Ceylon was an idyllic place to be stationed for a short time. He said morale was high and that conditions were relatively good compared to other places. He said boredom was the main problem and that the men called the Far East the "forgotten war." He supplied me with several books on the war in the Far East (now out of print) but was able to offer no clue to my father's mental or psychological state that might explain what happened.

• • •

By early 1943, Bill's letters were reflecting the boredom the veterans of Ceylon told me about. He felt his medicine was getting rusty, and he was itching to get back to feeling more useful in the war effort. He wrote to thank his parents for the Ray Ban sunglasses, coveted by everyone. Bill's constant lobbying for something more interesting to do was finally rewarded when Commander Scott wrote to London and recommended him for a course in the treatment of malaria at the Malaria Institute of India in Delhi.

On February 23, 1943 he wrote his parents about the course:

> Midwinter and I sit under an electric fan perspiring profusely as I write this letter…I'm going to a course on malariology in India. This should be most valuable even though the greater part of my life I may see little or no malaria….Of course what Ghandi and his followers do may affect the issue. At present it looks as if he is going to kill himself and, if he does, travel through India may be just a little too interesting over the next month or so.
>
> On Sunday I drove with Scotty and four others about 90 miles inland along a jungle trail—really a good road—into the heart

of the wilderness. Saw lots of deer and hundreds of large good-looking monkeys. Quite a few elephant tracks but saw no elephants. We are sending our men in groups out on jungle hikes now when they fend for themselves and pretty well live off the land. They stay out about five days and have a wonderful time. The English boys are not nearly so keen on it as the Canadians.

By the beginning of March, he was in Delhi and wrote his parents of his impressions:

Here I am with a new address at last, temporary though it is…I have come here for a course in malariology which should last a month and this apparently was a result of my repeated requests for a bit of practical work to do… I had four days to look over Delhi, both the old Delhi (where I live) which is dirty and squalid and Indian and the New Delhi which is clean, majestic and very pukka British, with all the good and evil which that latter phrase denotes.

Both Mr. Gandhi and the British Raj claim moral victories in their recent unarmed joust and I guess they are both right because they were both playing by different rules and gauged their victories by standards poles apart. So must it always be when the occidental meets the oriental, neither fathoming for an instant the workings of the mind of the other. How true Kipling was. It amazes me how well he understood this country from the pukka sahib (may I never be called one) to the regimental bhisti. But his day is gone and with it any vestige of respect for the Raj. The new free India? God knows. I can see nothing but confusion whether we stay in or move out and I don't know which would be worse.

The course is very specialized and keeps me working. The Malarial Institute of India is I suppose one of the first in the world and my colleagues are all Indians who have been suckled on malaria, which gives them a bit of an advantage…I start work at 7 and peer down microscopes or dissect mosquitoes til six daily except Sunday and swat at night so you can see it is like the good old days.

Just before his twenty-seventh birthday in April, Bill again wrote his parents, disappointed that he didn't come first in the exams:

I'm sure you are very anxious about my whereabouts and occupation and I am very sorry there has been this long silence…The malaria course was excellent—almost, I would say, the most engrossing weeks I have ever had…I ended up second in the examinations, being nosed out by a naval surgeon Lieutenant. I never seem to be able to make the top. I guess I haven't quite enough of what it takes. However, I was not too displeased with the result."

He had finally decided to take the RAF's offer of more interesting work in India. As a result, he returned to Ceylon after the course only to be told to pack his bags. He had a promotion to Senior Medical Officer, RAF Wing 172 near Madras on the southwest coast of India. His parish extended over hundreds of square miles and the job meant constant travelling.

I have stepped into the most chaotic disorganization that you could imagine. However, I have a job! At long last, I have a job of work to do.

He told the family back home the posting meant that he would not be coming home for a long time.

Life in Winnipeg must have seemed far away as Bill read a letter from his mother in June. She had just been to the wedding of Bill's old friend from university, Brian Dickson (later Chief Justice of the Supreme Court of Canada). *Brian and Barbara were married Friday. The former was sent home to take a course in Kingston.* She said it was a beautiful wedding and she thought of Bill when a toast was made to "the absent ones." News of Bill's promotion had reached Winnipeg. *Buzz* (Buzz B.) *took me to the guest pew and expressed satisfaction over your promotion. I was surprised he knew…*

Bill didn't write much that summer in India but, when he did, he sounded busy and much happier that the medicine was more serious.

On September 17, 1943 he wrote:

> 'So much to do, so little time to do it' applies aptly here. However, I would far prefer it this way than as it was in my last few months in Ceylon. I'm covering a pretty large territory...it's a grand experience and such a contrast to be fighting cholera, malaria and dysentery instead of pneumonia and T.B. It tends to give one a better perspective I think but when the happy day comes it will take a little while to get a grip on medicine in a temperate clime.
>
> The war news looks very bright and it looks as if Europe might conceivably be cleared up by next spring. Then it will be our turn and we are surely waiting for it.

Near the end of 1943, a letter arrived at South Drive from England. It gave a hint of some of the things Bill was leaving out of his letters home. I came across this letter during my search in a batch that was sent to me by a cousin who had saved some of my grandmother's things from South Drive.

The letter, dated November 3, 1943 was from P/O J. H. Coles, RAF Queen's Hotel, Harrowgate, Yorkshire, England and addressed to Mrs. J. H. Riley, South Drive. Coles had stayed with the Rileys when he was in Canada.

> Have you heard from Bill yet? I rather think he will be working like a slave now. The conditions in India are worse than anyone can possibly imagine and I am sure that this wholesale starvation will breed disease. As it is there are reports of cholera spreading in Bengal. Madras must also be suffering and medical aid is grossly inadequate. Only a fraction of the Indian news reaches the press but the silence is ominous. Unless a solution is arrived at fairly soon our offensive against Japan will be delayed indefinitely. It is very dangerous for Europeans to travel unarmed in many country districts. The whites are apparently

trying to distribute food evenly by way of rationing but the natives don't understand it and police discipline is non-existent. I believe that this partly explains Bill's failure to communicate with you. Your only worry need be for his health since he will be working harder than he has ever done now if conditions are as bad as I guessed.

But my father was determined to tell the family nothing of the conditions around him. When a letter from Bill finally arrived, dated October 31, 1943, it described a "glorious leave" at Ootacamund, 7,000 feet above sea level in the Nilgiri Hills. He had been invited as the guest of a Danish couple who owned a chalet in the hills.

I just eat and sleep and get sunburned and for these two weeks am enjoying myself more than at any time since I left home.

The letter is significant for the things left out.

Prior to coming up here I was very busy for various reasons that I can't very well discuss and I would write a book about it someday if there wasn't such a glut of very bad books about India already. No matter what the future holds, I will never regret my experiences in the East.

A copy of my father's New Testament from this period in India bears an inscription on the inside cover: *To Doc H. W. Riley with affectionate regards from The Bish, "The Lord bless thy going out and thy coming in from this time forth and forevermore". India, May 1943.*

In with these letters is a single sheet with a poem in Bill's handwriting, signed "Ootacamund November 1943" at the bottom. I have never found an author for the poem and am assuming my father wrote it.

O Death, thou poor and disappointed thing—
Strike if thou wilt, and soon, strike breast and brow,
For I have lived: and thou canst rob me now
Only of some long life that n'er has been,
The life that I have lived, so full, so keen,
Is mine! I hold it firm beneath thy blow
And, dying, take it with me where I go.

CHAPTER 11

HOMECOMING

I always wondered why, when he seemed committed to his job and determined to see his duty through, my father came home early, more than a year before the war ended. I was looking for clues that he was sick or perhaps showing signs of what was euphemistically called "shell shock" in World War I or "loss of nerve" in World War II and finally diagnosed as post-traumatic stress disorder (PTSD) after Viet Nam. I found none of that in a letter dated near the end of November 1943, in which Bill broke the sudden news to his parents that he was coming home.

> Well, it's happened or at least it is happening. I think you can plan to kill the fatted calf sometime early next year when the final thaw becomes well established. I had word from a Canadian chap at the Canadian liaison office at Delhi (an utterly ridiculous institution from our standpoint but useful for McKenzie King's publicity stunts) that Canada had signaled India requesting my return...I will leave India with regrets only exceeded by my desire to see you all. This is the last Christmas away. I know I said that last year...

He told the story this way to my mother.

> Sheila dearest, This is one of the happiest letters I have ever written.

He explained that he had been hearing rumors of a promotion for some time, a move which, he said, should mean another broad stripe on my shoulder. But, suddenly, there was a request from Ottawa to his RAF superiors.

> Two days ago a bombshell dropped in the form of a letter from a friend in Delhi who informed me that Canada has signalled India requesting my return forthwith.

This unofficial news really shook me to the core because, though nothing on the surface could be more attractive to me, it came at a bad time as such a move implied my losing my acting rank and facing the prospect of having to build up any reputation I may have achieved all over again in new surroundings. Still, everything considered, I did not feel I could make a formal protest as I might impair my chances of getting home for heaven knows how long. Yesterday, an official telephone message confirmed the previous note and my senior number was very unhappy about it. I did not know what to do. I knew that if I requested permission to stay, Air Headquarters here would back me up and Ottawa would probably defer. I was torn between my very real obligations here, for I owe a great deal to the RAF, and the immediate prospects of home and "je ne sais quoi."

Before my father had to make that choice, the Principal Medical Officer in India intervened on his behalf and asked RCAF London to postpone his posting to Canada for two months in order that he be confirmed as Squadron Leader, a rank he would never have qualified for back in Canada.

This letter is most egotistic and materialistic, he said and apologized. *My love to all the family both at home and abroad. I may have a chance of seeing Larry. Merry Christmas.*

A letter to the Commanding Officer of the Repatriation Depot in Ottawa confirmed that Squadron Leader Riley was being *retained in India two months for purpose of qualifying for temporary rank.*

Another letter from the RCAF Overseas Headquarters in London to the Defence Secretary in Ottawa, dated September 4, 1943 explained the sudden news that he was coming home:

This officer had requested a change of employment and in his application submitted the following statements:

"Prior to enlistment I graduated, with honours, from the University of Manitoba, receiving my M.D. degree in June, 1939

after a year's diversified internship at the Winnipeg General Hospital. The following year I spent as Resident in Medicine at the Winnipeg General Hospital and also held the appointment as Teaching Fellow in Medicine at the University of Manitoba. As an undergraduate, I had spent some months during vacations as a resident intern at the Provincial Psychiatric Hospital, Brandon. But for the intervention of the war, it had been my intention to continue post-graduate studies in internal medicine and psychiatry.

I make this application to request a posting either to a hospital, or to a junior position in connection with medicine and psychological problems arising in the Air Force, where experience could be obtained, under direction, in medicine or psychiatry. Such training, while obviously personally advantageous, should also greatly increase my value to the Air Force."

The letter concludes:

This officer is well reported on and is described as a very capable and able M.O. *who has worked hard and conscientiously. The case of this officer has been very carefully reviewed at this Headquarters and although his services could be used in the United Kingdom, it is felt that in view of his long service in India he should be returned to Canada for employment. Arrangements have been made to effect his repatriation at an early date.*

Next an RCAF Message, Cypher from South East Air Command copied to both RCAF in London and Ottawa:

SECRET. YOUR MICROGRAM LETTER A 297278/41 MAI 15 OCTOBER FLIGHT LIEUTENANT (A/S/L) HW RILEY CAN C 4069 MEDICAL EMBARKED FOR CANADA VIA SOUTH AFRICA 30 DECEMBER.

A telegram to Herbert Riley at Northern Trusts dated January 9, 1944:

"GREETINGS TO YOU ALL. DISCONTINUE MAIL."

A memo says he was repatriated and given disembarkation leave from February 4 to March 4, 1944. He was to report in Ottawa and then Winnipeg.

When Bill returned to Canada in January of 1944, Sheila's younger brother Larry was still in England. Bill wrote a rather formal letter to his young future brother-in-law telling him that he and Sheila were about to be married and asking for his blessing.

Larry replied to RCAF headquarters in Ottawa, but Bill didn't get the forwarded letter until weeks after the wedding, when he and Sheila were settled in Washington.

> *Your suggestion that I would want to "check up" on a future brother-in-law I found rather amusing. I have known you for quite a long time really, although I have not known you as well as I hope to, and I feel that the need for a check up is so distant as to be out of the question. I don't think that if I had looked all over Winnipeg, or even gone further afield, I could have found anyone who would, in my opinion, be so sure of making a perfect husband for Sheila than you.*

> *About your near and not too distant prospects you need not have said a word. Anyone who can do as well as you did in as difficult a profession as that of a doctor, first in Winnipeg and then in the air force need not fear for security. The fact that you survived what must be more than three years in the RCAF without losing ambition or initiative (a year and a half has destroyed what little I ever did have) and filled such a position as you did in India, makes me very proud of my brother-in-law.*

Larry was still overseas, waiting for the time when he, too, could return to Winnipeg. But his letter indicates that he didn't think he had any reason to worry about his sister Sheila and her impending marriage to Bill Riley.

• • •

My parents were married at All Saints Anglican Church in Winnipeg March 4, 1944. They had left the wedding until the last day of my father's leave and he was due in Washington right away. As it was still wartime, many friends and family were unable to attend. Larry was in England, Bill's sister Eleanor in Ottawa. A ceremony with reception at the Manitoba Club was arranged, Sheila's younger sister Lois remembers: *By this time I was in the Army at Camp Borden but came to Winnipeg to be bridesmaid. There was no chance to buy a dress so I wore my dress uniform and was pleased that Bill was also in uniform.* Bill's old friend Dr. Buzz B. was best man.

Right after the wedding, Sheila and Bill left Winnipeg by train.

A telegram dated March 4, 1944 arrived at South Drive.

PROCEEDING WASHINGTON TOGETHER ALL OUR BEST WISHES AND THANKS FOR EVERYTHING.

My parents were to go to Ottawa via Toronto and then to Washington where Bill was one of three Canadians enrolled in a course in tropical and military medicine run by the Army Medical School at Walter Reed Hospital. Sheila wrote the Rileys back home that *with the luxury of a drawing room, we scarcely knew the train was crowded.* They tried to see Eleanor, in Ottawa working for the National Film Board, but could not mesh schedules. They did manage to have lunch with Murray M. and his new bride, a nurse from Thunder Bay. Bill wrote his father from Washington on March 9. He sounded challenged and content:

> *My course is excellent. Certainly the best teachers and equipment available on this continent and in some ways the world. Your affectionate and very happy son, Bill*

In April, Sheila wrote Aunty Anne thanking her for helping with the wedding and for the housecoat, shoes and fur coat. She said Bill was working long hours but she had managed to find some work for a congressman so she was also keeping busy. Bill reported to his mother that, surprisingly, Sheila was a good cook.

The course went quickly and, by the end of April, Bill had his new orders. He was to proceed directly to No. 4 Training Command with headquarters in Calgary. They travelled by train from Washington via New York and this time visited Eleanor in Ottawa. Bill dropped Sheila in Winnipeg for a short visit with her parents and went straight to Calgary.

A letter dated May 2, 1944 from the Army Medical Center to the Director of the Medical Services for the RCAF in Ottawa reported that Bill had attained a grade of 94 out of 100 in the tropical medicine course. *This officer made an excellent impression, exhibiting outstanding qualities of accomplishment and leadership. Rating—Superior (highest rating given).*

By June, my parents were in the Palliser Hotel in Calgary. Bill wrote his father:

> *This has been a day of news with invasion reports coming in since early morning...it seems quite like the early days of the war but I hope it is the beginning of the end of it all...one feels very much out of it here.*

He added that he was bored with his job. *Some would say it's a cushy job but I don't like them too cushy.*

Sheila wrote to Mrs. Riley that they had found a furnished suite. The rent was high at $75.00 a month but Bill could walk to the hospital. She had heard that her parents had sold their house on Wardlaw and were to move. She and Bill had played golf and, although Bill was very rusty because he had not played in years, he did so well that they went again the next day. *Do I have to tell you whether we improved our scores?*

In December, Bill wrote his parents, describing his job as *presiding over the dissolution of a hospital in Calgary.* He said he was glad he was not involved in the dull toils of a release centre as many of his medical friends were, doing routine physicals. He said his chances of release from the RCAF were not good right then and that there was no sign of a posting to Winnipeg. He hinted he might have some prospects for a practice in Winnipeg and again expressed interest in psychiatry.

Gilbert Adamson suggested we may get involved in some of the "nervous breakdown" cases that are increasing all the time. I have always been interested in that sort of thing but I don't know if anything will come of it.

By this time, they knew Sheila was pregnant. Bill reported that she was feeling well but might want to be in Winnipeg in April when the baby was due.

She has been somewhat worried, Mother, by a reference in one of your letters to some uncertainty of her father's position. Please write me at work if you think that's advisable.

They later learned that my grandfather Gerald O'Grady had lost his job. It was a dreadful blow to the family and made money a constant worry for my grandparents. By the time my brother Michael Collum Riley was born April 16, my parents had returned to Winnipeg where Bill had been posted to the Joint Services Special Treatment Centre for Arthritis and Rheumatic Fever at Deer Lodge, a veterans' hospital. They rented a suite in the Milan apartments on McMillan Avenue while they looked for a house for their growing family.

It was in the Milan apartment that one of my grandmother Elsie's practical jokes entered family folklore. My grandmother and her best friend Fisher had long been known for their mischief. Michael was just a few months old and the new parents had not left him with anyone. Elsie offered to babysit while they went to a movie and Fisher joined her for company. When Sheila and Bill returned, they were met at the door by a distraught Elsie carrying a bundle with just a tuft of black hair showing under a corner of the blanket. She complained that the baby had screamed all night and, with that, threw her arms in the air in exasperation and the bundle went flying. The parents gasped as the contents revealed a rolled up newspaper and a shoebrush for hair. Fisher peeked around the corner from the bedroom, giggling. This story was repeated by many people with varying degrees of enthusiasm, but Elsie and Fisher were always delighted.

I learned from his official war record that Bill requested retirement from the RCAF in August, 1945 but was turned down with the explanation that his medical services were still required. In November, permission was granted based on the assurance that he had a chance to join an established medical practice in the new Winnipeg Clinic.

Within the year, Sheila was pregnant again, with me this time, and they moved to Waverley Street in River Heights, a central neighborhood in the Anglo-Saxon dominated south end of the city where the houses were large and the boulevards wide. Theirs was a four-bedroom two-storey with a sunroom off the living room on the south side, a solid red brick foundation and a fenced backyard where children could play.

For Sheila, it was finally the end of the "waiting life." She sat on the floor of the living room surrounded by cardboard cartons and discovered anew the joy of wedding presents, hurriedly packed away two years before. She held the Aynsley bone china tea cups up to the light, one by one. The Wicker Lane coffee cups and dessert plates soon formed a circle around her on the hardwood floor, an imaginary dining table. Here was a wooden salad bowl she had forgotten, twelve silver teaspoons from her old boss at Great-West Life, eight Georgian coffee spoons from Murray M. She rose awkwardly, teetering under the weight of the pregnancy, to hang the mirror framed in mahogany on a random picture hook left by the previous owners. She looked at herself in the glass and smiled. It had been a busy year and she was tired but happy.

I, Susan Patton Riley, arrived November 6, 1946, the *Winnipeg Tribune* reported. My parents hired Amy to help with what was now two children. By the spring of 1947, Michael was a busy two-year-old and I was sitting up on my own. Michael smashed the nail of his middle finger in the garage door but, other than that, the family seemed to survive the Winnipeg winter. Bill was busy establishing a practice at the Winnipeg Clinic and Sheila volunteered at the Junior League.

The photo albums I have are filled with baby pictures in the Waverley house and backyard. Michael had matured into a plump blonde active toddler. I am also in the pictures, hair rising into a peculiar tuft on the top of my head. My hair was bright red from birth, a subject of many jokes in the hospital. Bill's doctor friends wondered where the redhead came from. Rileys didn't have that colouring but, fortunately, there was red hair on the O'Grady side to explain me.

There are a few black and white snapshots of my father with baby Michael but none of my father with me. The last series of family photographs, before they abruptly stop, is a group taken at Matlock on Lake Winnipeg. It was a weekend toward the end of August 1947 and Sheila, Bill and their two children went to Matlock to spend the weekend with Marge and Art Johnston and their two children at the cottage. Marge Johnston, my godmother, was an old friend of Sheila's from high school and university.

While the children played on a blanket in the shade, the adults lazily watched a couple of crows perched on a barbed wire fence nearby. Marge studied one of the crows in profile, black feathers glistening in the sun. Then she looked back to study Bill Riley, sitting beside her.

"Turn sideways, Bill," she commanded. Bill, seeing what was coming, preened in profile for her. The others looked too.

"You look exactly like that crow when you turn that way."

"Thanks a lot," said Bill and they all laughed.

These brief vignettes from the married life of my parents were gleaned from letters, newspaper clippings, family photographs and stories told to me many years later, along with some imagined scenes. It was not much with which to build a childhood with my father. In the meantime, I was drawing strength from a new friendship with an old friend of my mother's.

CHAPTER 12

"DON'T WATCH THE WAVES"

FALL, 1987

L ess than six months after my mother died, when I was 41, I stepped off the Tiger Air shuttle bus that had taken me the two-hour drive from St. Louis to Columbia, Missouri. I searched the strip mall parking lot where I was supposed to meet Marty. I was looking for the tall, athletic tennis player in shorts and a T-shirt with a carefree stance that signaled independence. That was what I remembered from the pictures. Instead, driving the navy '68 Camaro V-8, barely visible over the steering wheel, was a white-haired, old woman. From the back seat a golden cocker spaniel peered through the window. I was soon leaning over to hug Marty, now a short, plump but sturdy seventy-eight year old with wrinkled skin, darkened by sun spots. Lively intelligent eyes twinkled behind her thick glasses.

She drove, alarmingly fast, to her house that hung on a ravine on the top of a hill surrounded by old walnut trees and tall pines. Marty's home was a natural retreat like a log cabin in the woods—only hers was all wood, brick and glass. Wooden and wrought iron chairs and benches on the stone patios on either side of the house faced the hill overlooking the creek below. A screened-in porch was suspended over the ravine like a room in the treetops. Although the house was modern, designed by a famous architect, it was filled with traditional furniture and paintings Marty had collected on her teaching trips around the world. In the living room comfortable armchairs provided a sunny spot in front of floor-to-ceiling windows in the corner.

Over the next few years, this place became my escape from Winnipeg. As I began to change my life in my forties, Columbia, Missouri, was a place I could be myself without worrying about what others thought or expected. Marty lived all her life as a single person, always earned her own living and had, as a result, become independent both by instinct and necessity. She had assembled a collection of women friends, slightly eccentric but definitely not conservative or judgmental. It occurred to me later as I read my parents' letters that both, at times, had also been looking for an escape from the claustrophobic Winnipeg society they grew up in. Sheila, when she first settled in Kamaji, noticed how much freer and less inhibited she felt at camp. Part of her release was no doubt due to the friendship of Marty, a woman who, even early in life, had no time for the expectations of others. Bill also seemed to enjoy the freedom of travel far from home, opening up to other cultures and ways of life.

When Marty and I were settled in the chairs that Molly the dog had grudgingly vacated for us, we talked about Sheila. "You have her eyes," Marty said. Over the next two days, I told her about Sheila's life after they lost touch with one another.

"It's something I will always regret and I don't really know how it happened. Just busy lives and distance, I suppose," she said. Marty didn't even know what Sheila's last name became after her second marriage in 1954. "At one time I thought of advertising in a Winnipeg paper to find her but, obviously, I didn't." If Marty thought it odd that Sheila O'Grady's daughter would turn up after all these years, travelling hundreds of miles from Canada to visit, she never let on. When I think back, I know that I needed this living proof of my mother's past life, a confirmation of who she was, but I also realize now that Marty needed it too, a kind of second chance to continue a friendship that had slipped away.

I told her about Sheila's years with Alzheimer's, the early ones when the doctors didn't know why she was losing her memory and the final diagnosis of a disease we had never heard of. By then my mother couldn't dress or feed herself. She had for years been writing notes to herself in an effort to remember people she felt she should know. I remember finding little crumpled-up pieces of paper beside her bed with names printed on a list after she had been to a dinner party. She fooled a lot of people with her gentle grace and charm when she didn't have a clue who they were. Larry said she even did it to him, her brother, the last time he saw her in the nursing home in St. Norbert. "Oh, hello," she said with a sweet smile, pretending to know who he was.

In her turn, Marty told me about the past and my young mother—how laughter was what had brought them together. Marty had gone to Camp Kamaji as a child and, later, when she needed a summer job, had taught tennis there for a number of summers, supplementing the salary she earned from teaching at Stephens, which was really only an eight-month-a-year job. She remembered in the summer of 1941 how a young sailing instructor was introduced to the campers—Sheila O'Grady, from Winnipeg, Canada. Sheila was twenty-three and it was her first job away from home. Marty was thirty-four and had been away from her childhood home in LeMars, Iowa for over a decade.

"There is to be no visiting after curfew at nine o'clock. Young ladies need their beauty sleep," intoned Bert, the camp director, as the new employees gathered for a recitation of the rules. Sheila caught Marty's eye and they both started to giggle. They couldn't stop. Trying to make a good impression, Sheila bit her lip. But Marty, who had known Bert and Phil for years, didn't care and laughed out loud.

Years later, Marty would write to Sheila that *they are two of the screwiest females I have ever encountered and I certainly don't pretend to understand them.* That was in the days when Marty was counting on a summer job at the camp and Bert and Phil were reluctant to offer her one. Bert and Phil did well promoting Kamaji to wealthy families as a place to send their daughters for a few weeks to learn skills for the life of luxury their parents hoped they would someday lead. These young women learned tennis and sailing and maybe a few wilderness tricks, perhaps how to make a fire. But the word "lesbian" was never spoken at Kamaji. Bert and Phil were careful of their reputation among the traditional conservatives who made up their market and Marty was unconventional enough to worry them. She didn't always do as she was told. She would probably have a bad influence on the young Canadian and Bert and Phil thought they should be kept apart.

But Sheila and Marty became friends. They played tennis and went for long walks in their time off. Marty, who grew up in the American Corn Belt, had never been sailing. Although Sheila lived on the eastern edge of the Canadian Prairie, she had sailed since she could walk. Her grandfather "Skipper" Patton had been an avid sailor and tethered a thirty-two-foot sailboat to a buoy in front of his camp. Sheila learned to sail from her mother and her mother's brothers who won cups at the Royal Lake of the Woods Yacht Club. Her name was also on some of those cups at the yacht club for both sailing and diving, cups that would end up in my wooden box of family things.

My mother instructed Marty, "Don't watch the waves. They won't tell you where the wind is." Sheila showed her how to tie a tell-tail from the top of the mast so that she didn't have to find a flag or hold a wet finger up to find out the wind direction. "See, the wind is coming from there so we should be able to tack upwind and head for the far shore," Sheila said, pointing. Back and forth they skimmed over the water with just the sound of the wind and the waves. It was freeing and Marty loved it.

One day at the end of July, Marty got a call from LeMars. Her father had suffered a stroke and died. The first bus back home to Iowa didn't leave until morning. She found Sheila and they wandered down to sit on the dock in the late evening. As the sun sank over the lake and spread purple across the sky, they talked and talked, about their lives, their families, and death. Their friendship was cemented that night on the dock. "Your mother was beautiful and loving that night when I felt so lost," Marty remembered.

When Bert and Phil discovered that the two camp instructors had spent the night on the dock, they were furious. "What will people think?" they asked. Marty didn't care.

• • •

As I climbed back into the Tiger Air shuttle after that first visit, with the lunch Marty had made me carefully wrapped in wax paper packages, I knew this was the beginning of an important new friendship, in a sense a continuation of an interrupted one from the past.

When I got back to Winnipeg, I began to share important things with Marty by letter. One September afternoon, my brother Mike and I drove to Keewatin on a blustery day and took the boat out to the yacht club stretch where our mother had sailed for so many years. Together, we held the small glass jar and scattered her ashes on the water. The wind lifted and spread them before they hit the surface. We silently watched the waves for a while as the ashes disappeared under the foam. Then we drove back to shore. I wrote Marty about this little ritual. She seemed the obvious one to share this moment with.

Marty and I wrote often after my first visit. It was not unusual to get a letter from her when she was well into her eighties with the report: *I played tennis this week.* Served a couple of aces. If Marty did not seem to be aging, Molly was. She became blind in one eye and she eventually lost sight in the other. Marty gave her the best of care. The dog survived for some time with no sight, having memorized the places she needed to go in the house. But, in May of 1992, Marty had to put Molly down. By June, she had convinced a breeder to let her have a five-month-old Springer spaniel. The breeder, who was extremely careful about whom she approved as owners, was reluctant to let an eighty-three-year-old woman have one of her dogs, but Marty talked her into it by promising that she would see to it that the dog was always looked after. Muffin was at first to be called Murphy after the tough-talking television journalist in the TV series Murphy Brown but she just *seemed to be more of a Muffin*, Marty wrote. Prophetically, she wrote that spring of 1992 that Muffin liked playing in snow, a rare sight in Missouri but this time delivered by a freak storm.

I was forty-one when I first found Marty. I had been married for 17 years and my children were in their early teens. In our first few visits, Marty was teaching me that it was possible for a woman to live on her own, to be independent and fulfilled. It was not something I had learned yet and she didn't even know she was teaching it. She was healthy and had a group of friends around her. She walked Molly, and later Muffin, every day, and every week it seemed there was some event to look forward to. Friends dropped by and they took turns hosting the football evenings and looking after each other's pets when one of them travelled. Marty actually lived in a community and this group of friends and neighbours looked after her as she aged and enabled her to feel safe living on her own.

We had talked obliquely about sexuality over the years, and I had come to know that, although non-judgmental about such things, Marty was sober about how many people in society treated the subject. She advised caution. When I told her I was in love with a woman, she was not surprised but told me bluntly to be careful. She worried about the effect on my children and my career. She had seen a lot of academics ruin their career over the issue and said there was a phobia in women's colleges. "Don't make an announcement," she said. "Heterosexuals don't announce that they are heterosexual. Why should gay people?" She had counselled students to be cautious in leaping into something that seemed so new and exciting and overwhelming. Sometimes it was only an experiment, sometimes it didn't work out and there were risks in acting too quickly.

This was good advice and carried me through difficult times when I was confused and when the children were young and vulnerable to society's views. When I finally met my partner Rhonda, we drove to Missouri so that she could meet Marty. They were both teachers, loved dogs and had a similar sense of humour. One of the first things Marty said to Rhonda when I was unloading the Jeep was: "My land, Susan looks so much like her mother."

I had brought Marty a copy of Sheila's diary that described the importance of their friendship after the summer of 1941 and I gave it to her to read. One night after we had gone to bed in Marty's bedroom, I got up in the dark. In the living room below, Marty was sitting on the couch, the light from the reading lamp over her shoulder illuminating the diary, with tears in her eyes. I did not disturb her.

CHAPTER 13

LARRY'S WAR

As I began to pursue the story of my parents, at first I forgot about asking Uncle Larry anything, even though he had been the last person to see my father alive. I had not seen him since my mother's funeral in 1987 and had heard very little news of him. Although he had been our favorite uncle when we were growing up, we had lost touch when he moved to Vancouver. In 1960, Larry had married Bev, who had lived all her life on the West Coast. Neither Sheila nor Lois was able to go to the wedding. Over the years, Larry and Bev visited the O'Grady camp at Keewatin bringing their white standard poodle named Punch and their adopted son who, even at age six, was beyond the control of his parents. He was later diagnosed as an extreme paranoid schizophrenic. Larry's wife Bev had long blond hair and wore full-length summer dresses and wide-brimmed straw hats when everyone else was in shorts or jeans. Sheila and Lois always had the feeling that she thought she was better than everyone else in the O'Grady family.

In his younger years, Larry had been very close to my mother. My memory box offered up many letters he had sent Sheila during the war while he was serving overseas. By the end of 1943, in her "waiting time," my mother was writing both to Bill in India and to Larry in England and she saved many of their replies. Larry's age, qualifications, experience and personality meant his war years were very different from my father's, although both were in the air force.

When war was declared in September 1939, Larry was still in high school. By the time he turned eighteen in 1942, the war was going badly for the Allies and there was no question in Larry's mind but that he would have to enlist. He was not naive about war and had none of the romantic notions of many of his generation. He was aware of what war had done to his father. In addition to the physical wounds, Larry sensed that his father had deep psychological scars from his service in World War I. He thought his father would have been happier and had a more successful life without war. Gerald deCourcy O'Grady senior graduated from Upper Canada College, became a lawyer and then went into business. But then he lost his job and ended his working days unhappily trying to sell insurance. He drank too much and never talked to his children about the war.

So young Larry O'Grady decided he wanted none of the mud, cold and filth he associated with life in the army. He was no more attracted to the thought of a watery death at sea; therefore, he opted for the new and relatively unknown prospect of service in the air force. He thought that death, if it came, would be quick and clean. He signed up, became a bomber pilot and was sent overseas to be stationed near London at Lancaster. He and many other Canadian men spent their nights flying bomber missions over occupied Europe. Although he had rejected the army and the navy at least partly because he wanted to outlive the war, it turned out that the casualty rate for the aircrews doing this work was many times higher than that in most jobs in the other forces. Air force experts had set a "tour" in bomber command at thirty trips. That meant that these young pilots had a slim chance of surviving thirty forays over German occupied territory. But most of them, like Larry, felt that they were invincible and, even though they had seen comrades shot out of the sky countless times, they still thought that fate was for "the other guy." Larry later talked about some close calls on bombing missions when he seriously feared for his life. *Although I did face fearsome dangers, I have always felt very guilty about the part I played in World War II because I thoroughly enjoyed most of my time in the war.*

Larry's letters home during the war—like my father's—never mentioned the danger. He wrote Sheila to thank her for the fudge (*I hope you have some sugar left*) and the black knitted socks. He told her he was getting nearly four hours of flying a day, only in Moths, although there were rumors they might get some Cornels at the end of the month. He wished the family dog could be with him to go running as he had heard Patrick had been getting a little fat lately.

In November of 1943, he wrote Sheila, gently teasing about her misconceptions regarding what his life might be like. He said any chance of seeing something of historical England was unlikely as he only got one day off a week and had no chance to get off the base. He addressed her concern that he might get married by pointing out that his matrimonial prospects were nil. Then he spent a long time on the weather (*not as bad or as cold as expected*) and the food (*same as the weather*) and told her not to let Jacky get fat and to pay attention to Patrick. The family dogs were always a safe subject.

When the war was over, Larry returned to Canada and lived with his parents in Winnipeg while he completed a Commerce degree at the University of Manitoba. After university, Larry began work at the Hudson's Bay Company in the ladies suits and coats department.

• • •

One afternoon in May of 1992, Uncle Larry came back into my life with force. My brother Mike called my office in a panic. He didn't know details but Uncle Larry had been charged in Vancouver with the murder of his wife, Bev. Neither of us could believe it. Larry had always been a risk taker, rich one day and broke the next, but nothing about his life had ever indicated that he was capable of the violence involved in the brutal stabbing of Bev. However, we had been out of touch for a long time and we knew that all lives take twists and turns.

We followed the seven-year battle in the B.C. courts from Winnipeg. Larry steadfastly proclaimed his innocence, but he refused to cast any blame on the schizophrenic adopted son who lived just around the corner. As a result, the defence's case was slim. After three trials for second-degree murder, the last appeal was rejected in March of 1999. Larry was sentenced to life in prison with parole eligibility after 10 years. It was a crushing blow for the family: we had always believed that his appeals would be successful. Larry began his 10-year mandatory sentence at the Mission Institute, a medium security federal prison an hour northeast of Vancouver.

But he could receive and write letters. When I remembered that Larry had been in the car on the drive that night from Keewatin, I wrote to him in prison. I had given up, deciding that, like all the others, he didn't really want to talk about my father, when a letter arrived with a "Mission Institute" return address.

Dear Susan,

The following will be a bit rambling and not very organized but it will give you a bit of a picture of what I might be able to do and what I don't think I can do (at present).

…Bill gave my father and me a ride back from the lake in his car that Sunday night. We left after dinner at approximately 6:30 pm. About half way home, Bill asked me if I would like to drive so I drove the rest of the way to 889 Grosvenor Avenue. There was nothing unusual about this. Many people make this procedure a habit. Traffic was fairly heavy and a bit slow. We got to our house at ten or ten thirty pm.

Dad invited Bill in for a nightcap but he declined. Nothing unexpected about this. It was not late and we would be able to get a good night's sleep before the coming work week.

The trip back had been completely relaxed and uneventful with just the normal conversation between the three of us. I can remember nothing of this talk now but at the time I played it back and forth in my mind over and over for weeks and could never find anything that seemed unusual or wrong.

I believe it was the following Tuesday when Mr. Riley phoned me at work and told me that he was very worried about Bill.

A while later Mr. Riley phoned me, gave me the dreadful news and asked me if I would meet him at the house. The police were still there and (either at their suggestion or my request, I'm not sure) I viewed Bill. (Susan, if you want more details re this I will of course send them to you).

Larry then said both he and Mr. Riley questioned the police and satisfied themselves that "it would have been impossible for anyone else to have been in the house and leave it locked the way they found it."

> Mr. Riley then asked me if I would drive down to the lake and tell Sheila. This I did and it was the most ghastly thing I have ever done. I'd composed a sort of a speech on the way down but it flew out the window when I was face to face with Sheila and I'm afraid I just blurted out the facts.
>
> Since then I have given things a great deal of thought but have never been able to arrive at any plausible conclusion as to why this thing happened...

Then he had to try to do what I had asked and describe my father to me.

> I knew Bill fairly well although my knowledge of him was somewhat limited because I only knew him for a relatively short time and usually saw him in the company of Sheila and my parents and other relatives. Nevertheless, I think I can do a reasonably good job of portraying Bill as a decent man, intelligent, well liked, easy to know. He was really at the start of what promised to be a very good life. He had a beautiful wife and two lovely children, a nice house and what could only turn out to be an excellent medical practice. I believe I would have heard something if there were any problems in Bill's marriage, medical practice or business affairs.
>
> Unfortunately, although Bill and I did have some quiet moments together, we never got around to discussing our war experiences. This is not surprising since, although we were both in the air force, there was little similarity in our services. I was in the air crew in England and he was in the medical arm in the Far East. Very different.

This was the beginning of many more exchanges Larry and I would have about the war and its effects on people. His reflections on Bill as a person in this first letter were careful and, I assumed, cautious because he was worried about the impact details might have on me. I would later learn more about his feelings and why he held back.

But then he turned to the subject he needed to talk about—Sheila. He needed to know that we knew her story as he knew it and he needed to express the hurt and rage he had held in for all those years.

> If I could deal adequately with Bill's tragedy I could also deal with your and your mother's and Michael's tragedy. These certainly should be part of the story. I think they should, although perhaps Sheila's story deserves a space of its own...
>
> For someone who was head girl of her school, a top athlete at basketball, swimming, fancy diver and even a public performer at ballet, who waltzed through university with top marks with only a minimum of studying and who got one of the top secretarial jobs in the city (without knowing typing or shorthand) and then suddenly became a little old befuddled lady, starting at about the age of forty-five is stupefying. The complete story on Alzheimer's is not yet written. I wonder if they will discover that bereavement, heartbreak and stress can accelerate the disease?
>
> Susan, you were very young at the time but can you remember when you and Michael lived in the top of the Riley house with your mother? Sheila was worried about the disturbance two playful young children could cause so she kept you quiet by reading to you for hours every morning...She did this very willingly even though I know that, on top of everything else, it was very stressful for her.

In this first letter, Larry also apologized for not doing more and referred to "minimal capabilities in here." That first letter was handwritten. He later got access to a computer. I was now emotionally prepared for more and wrote asking Larry for the facts about Bill's death he had said he had.

In his next letter, Larry first wanted to expel any thoughts of murder. He was sure in his own mind that it was suicide. *Mr. Riley found the house locked and tried but could not get in. The police said it could not have been locked by anyone leaving the house. This would have been a fairly simple thing for them to determine.*

I reminded Larry that he himself must know that the police will sometimes take the easy route and are driven by a need to wrap things up quickly and neatly. But he was firm in the opinion that he had had many years to explore and wrestle with this, and he assured me that he believed he was right. I always suspected in my investigation that people were holding things back, either because they themselves were uncomfortable with the taboos I wanted to talk about or because they genuinely believed that they were protecting me from things that would hurt me. I accused Larry of the same. He insisted that he was holding nothing back and was not lying or hiding anything. It was clearly difficult for him to go back to that scene he was forced to witness as a young man of 24. But he had to explain his certainty to me now. *It was not a gory scene but even over 50 years later I find it a scene which I would give a lot to erase from my memory.* It was not until I insisted that he finally described what he had seen. I had by this time sent him a copy of the autopsy, which he did not know existed and some of Bill's letters home from the war.

I believe, he wrote in July, 2001, *you have hit on the main reason I am firmly of the opinion that this was suicide while Bill was not in full and proper control of his faculties and that murder was not a factor.*

> *Bill was dressed in a pair of air force pants and a navy blue sleeveless woolen sweater. He was in a shower in the basement, draped across the floor of the shower and partially up the far corner shower walls. The revolver was lying on the floor of the shower. It was not a gory scene: I did not see the wound.*

> *What decided me was the sweater. It seems a little unusual that Bill would have air force pants on, but it is absolutely not credible that normally Bill would have ever put on this sweater without a shirt underneath. I had one of those sweaters but never*

wore it. They were not air force issue but were sent to us by women at home. They were woolen, hand knit and sleeveless. Firstly, I would never put a sleeveless woolen sweater on without a shirt underneath and secondly, I would never put one on which was as scratchy and itchy as these were. My conclusion is that Bill's clothing is a clear indication that he dressed himself while he was not in a sound frame of mind. My second conclusion is that it is extremely unlikely that any second party would choose: a) air force attire b) clothing items that are so bizarre, sleeveless sweater in the summer over no shirt c) clothing items that are not readily at hand but are away at the bottom of the furthest drawers or at the bottom or back of closets, probably under other clothing.

I had, in my letters, provided Larry with a lot of information he had not had—the autopsy, some war letters, the official cause of death and some of the speculation we had picked up from people in Winnipeg who had been around at the time. I also told him about letters from Lois in Montreal and her discussions with Sheila about murder. But Larry's mind was made up now and he communicated his conclusions to me and to Lois. He was convinced that the war years had taken their toll. He said the "letters home" were not indicative of what was really going on. He himself picked up clues from the letters that showed things were worse than they seemed.

These "letters home" were always written the same way. They were all as light and amusing and interesting as we could make them and we never said that our quarters were damp and cold, our food was poor and that we were tired and discouraged and homesick and lonely and that we were scared and had a premonition that our time had come.

He also talked about Bill's sensitivity. Bill once told him a story about his work as a doctor in Winnipeg that made an impression on Larry for years afterwards. Bill was called by a company that used him as doctor to go to the factory and see the foreman. The foreman showed him a machine on the assembly line and told him about the worker who had misused the machine and cut off two of his fingers. The foreman, while showing Bill how it had happened, promptly cut off two of his own fingers.

Bill told me how he felt and what a dreadful thing it had been and I agreed because I felt the same way. But, at the time I wondered if Bill had overreacted. Although I agree that a doctor is not a very good one if he loses empathy and sympathy for his patients, I also think that a doctor is courting trouble if he suffers as deeply as Bill seemed to suffer.

I also asked Larry about a story of Grandfather Riley throwing the gun found in the shower off the Maryland Bridge. Larry said he had not heard that but was not surprised. His reasoning was that it was a sensible way to get rid of something you would not want to keep. The police didn't need it anymore. The case was closed.

Larry, with my help, had come to the conclusion that Bill had a tropical disease—probably malaria—that he had been self-medicating and perhaps became addicted to some drug used to treat the disease. He then killed himself, perhaps in a delusional state caused by the drugs. The pieces were not fitting together as well for me, but Larry seemed more and more certain. He also was convincing his sister Lois through phone calls and letters to Montreal. It was not until I decided to go and visit Larry that I discovered why it was important for him to learn more about what happened to Bill.

CHAPTER 14

LARRY'S LAST RESORT

"Stick close to me. You have to wait till you hear the lock click," she said.

On the click she opened the door but not before the one behind us clanked shut. As I fought off my claustrophobia, we moved together through the last door and into a room much like a cafeteria with tables bolted to the floor and chairs around them. Already most of the visitors were scattered at various tables. "He'll come through that door," she said, pointing. "It sometimes takes a little while but they'll let him know you're here." I sat at an empty table beside the soft drink machine where I could watch the door. Three guards sat in an area behind glass with microphones in front of them. A play place with toys and a climbing apparatus was in one corner but no children were playing.

My unofficial guide, the woman with bright orange spiky hair and high heels who had helped me through the doors, greeted her brother. He was heavyset, over six feet tall and immediately enclosed her in burly arms. His grey hair fell in greasy strands over his shoulders and a beaded band circled his forehead. Larry later told me that this man had organized a prison riot and was therefore held in some regard.

As the couple at the table next to me held hands and kissed, I began to wonder if anyone had told Larry I was coming. The woman on the phone this morning had been curt and would not confirm whether I was on the visitor list. Then the door opened. Uncle Larry shuffled in, stood still and looked uncertainly around the room. He was wearing cheap running shoes, blue jeans and a worn red ski jacket, hanging loosely on his shoulders. I stood up and started to walk forward so he could see me. He smiled.

That smile. Memories flooded back of the handsome young bachelor, my mother's younger brother, our favorite uncle, the one who could always make us giggle. Uncle Larry had blond hair, soft blue eyes, a red Alpha Romeo Giulietta Sprint sports car and lots of glamorous girlfriends. He had been a bomber pilot in the war and we had a picture of him, still a teenager, standing in front of "his" plane in England, his air force hat set at a jaunty angle. I guess my brother Mike and I must have bothered him when we were kids because we had to be told not to hang around his cabin next door (called Larry's Last Resort) without permission when he had visitors. He had lots of visitors, most of them young women. He had loud parties and friends who water-skied dangerously close to the dock, snatching a beer off the diving board on the way by. This seemed a lot more fun to Mike and me than the things we did with our widowed mother and grandparents.

The Uncle Larry I sat with in the visitor room at the Mission Correctional Institute, in Mission, British Columbia that Saturday afternoon was seventy-eight. His grey hair was thinning on the top but he appeared fit and healthy. He told me he worked out every day and held a full-time job in the prison office. He had practiced meditation long before he came here and that had allowed him to survive in this place. His grin was still mischievous; it implied we shared a secret joke.

I had not seen him since my mother's funeral in Winnipeg. We both knew we had a lot to do in the two three-hour visits we had been able to arrange this weekend but we also needed to have fun. We were soon laughing about the time Uncle Eric made a waterproof channel by rolling up the edge of the oilcloth covering the cottage dining table and watched as water dripped into the lap of a pompous guest at the far end. When I told him I heard that his grandfather Patton got electricity in the cottage only after his grandmother died when her hair caught fire in a coal oil lamp, he asked innocently: "Isn't that a bit like closing the barn door?" He was gleeful when he heard that his sisters Sheila and Lois fumed when their mother Elsie crowed about her "wonderful letter from Larry." The sisters were stuck caring for elderly parents in poor health in Winnipeg and a few lines from Larry in Vancouver was all it took to give Elsie a conversation topic for months. Those were not "wonderful" letters, he confirmed, but he still took fiendish delight in their effect on his sisters.

It was Larry who turned to the reason I was here. "You probably have been wondering," he said, "why it took me so long to reply to your letter." Tears filled his eyes and he had to pause. "I had a lot of anger about what Bill did to Sheila and I didn't know if I could answer you without showing it."

He said he had always prided himself for being a non-judgmental person but he found himself unable to feel any sympathy for the man who had betrayed his sister. "I simply could not forgive him for leaving her and leaving you two. She worked so hard to be a good parent but those early days living with the Rileys were not easy. And I felt more and more sure that her deterioration later in life was caused by the shock and grief after his death," he told me as we talked in the prison that day.

Now I was offering him a way to feel some empathy for the brother-in-law he wanted to forgive. Larry had been thinking a lot about the sacrifices of war, of his father's, of his many contemporaries' who had never been the same and of Bill Riley's. He told me a story of his friend Dave who returned from the war to marry the girl of his dreams. She was blond and beautiful and they soon had three little blond children. But Dave couldn't make it work. He seemed to have it all and yet he drank it away. He lost his job, lost his wife and children, and then disappeared. Larry was always puzzled by Dave. In prison he found himself thinking about him a great deal. Then I came along with my questions about Bill Riley and he started to make a connection. He had read about post-traumatic stress disorder and its effect on Viet Nam war veterans. He was sure he had seen the same in veterans of the world wars—they just didn't have a name for it then.

Larry and I had a good visit. We talked about his case and any chance for appeal or early release, more about Bill and Sheila, but we also found time to laugh at old family jokes. When I returned to Winnipeg, he wrote to thank me for having the courage to open old wounds. He said he and Lois had reached a kind of closure and hoped I had found some sort of peace.

I must tell you how much I enjoyed your visits here. I can't remember having so much fun in two days and yet I felt we accomplished some things of real value…it is true that one of my objectives was to bring some closure to you and I am very glad that we have been partially successful in this and I am sure that time will continue this process. However, I was not completely unselfish in this endeavor. I also had in mind Lois and myself. Although our pain was miniscule in comparison to yours, we nevertheless were badly hurt by Bill's death and the terrible questions it raised. This leaves out Sheila and Bill; although we can do nothing for them now, we can do something about our memories of them. I, for one, feel as though a heavy weight has been lifted from me because I now understand what happened to Bill or what probably happened to Bill.

I, on the other hand, was not nearly so sure as Larry seemed to be.

● ● ●

Part of Larry's story will never be told. He died still a prisoner one Thanksgiving weekend and his many efforts to appeal ended with his death. In all his attempts to prove his innocence, he did not raise evidence showing that, at the time of the murder, his son, a diagnosed paranoid schizophrenic, had a history of difficulty with his mother and had just found out the upsetting news that he was adopted. Larry remained convinced that the prison system was not a good place for the mentally ill and he made sure his son was cared for in a good group home nearby and that they had regular visits.

Following his death, in a memorial service in the chapel at the federal penitentiary, inmates packed the room and rose, one by one, to give tributes to Larry, a man they knew only as their teacher of English and creative writing. After the service, Larry's family was able to meet with long-time convicts who talked about how Larry had changed their lives. We listened to poetry the inmates had written for his class and discovered a world we had not known existed behind those walls. The stories helped his family deal with his death after seven years in a federal penitentiary. They helped us understand that Larry had used his time in prison to help others and made what we saw as his sacrifice seem a little less futile. At the same time I remembered how generous Larry had been when my questions about my father arrived in his prison cell by letter. Even in the medium security penitentiary when he didn't have use of a computer, he carefully wrote out longhand answers to my questions, returning to what was for him as a young man, a painful time. He said he hoped his efforts would begin to bring about at least some closure and I think they did.

CHAPTER 15

MUSICAL EVENINGS

The new information from Uncle Larry propelled my search for what happened to my father to a new level. I gained more confidence to speak about what I had before regarded as unspeakable. My talks with Larry showed me how valuable first person accounts become when trying to reconstruct history. The official documents—like the war record from Veterans Affairs or the autopsy report—could never reveal that my father had been wearing military clothing when he was found. The descriptions of the death scene could only come from someone who was there and Uncle Larry was the only one left. At first, the military clothing seemed important as a concrete signal that his death was connected with the war. It sent me back to the war years and my search for people who had known him then. But, as I began to talk to them, I did not seem to be getting any closer to a reason for his death. Larry was becoming more and more convinced that his theories about post traumatic stress from the war years or some medical problem related to drugs was the answer and was trying to persuade me to accept the explanation and move on. But, as I found more out about the war years, I was not convinced that we had the answer. The mystery only grew.

Besides telling me about his death, Uncle Larry had also been able to talk to me about my Dad's life, what he was like as a person. Speaking to him had made me bolder about trying to search for others who had known my Dad. I began methodically to search for anyone still alive who might have known him. In the past, the discomfort people showed in talking about suicide made it difficult to raise the topic casually in conversation. I always had the feeling people worried about me whenever I wanted to talk about my father. They had good reason to avoid the subject. Those close to my mother were probably filled with anger and hurt. And those who knew my father better were at a loss to explain behavior so out of character and, therefore, didn't know what to say to his daughter. After my talks with Larry, I began to approach the story as a journalist, compiling a list of anyone who had mentioned my father to me in the past and people I didn't know who might have something to add. I phoned, wrote letters and e-mailed anyone I could think of. Before that, my search had only been through casual, unorganized questioning.

I had already begun the legal research, the collection of officially available documents. They trickled in over the years, the speed depending on how easy they were to release, with new privacy legislation. It was only when I had received all the documents—from the medical examiners office, the pathology department at the hospital, records at the Winnipeg Clinic, his entire war record from Veterans Affairs—and talked to Uncle Larry, supposedly the last person to see him alive—that it became clear that the various stories I had been told did not fit together.

When people talked to me about my father in the past, references had always been made to the war. The various stories from different people over the years speculated that he was never the same when he came back from the Far East, that he had had an inoperable brain tumor, that financial matters might have been involved, that he may have been in trouble with drugs. The one that made the most sense—and the one that Larry supported—was the idea that he had contracted malaria when he was in India treating patients with tropical diseases and that he had never recovered. The theory was that he had self medicated and eventually either overdosed or tried to quit. This theory purported that he had killed himself during an episode of either drug-induced depression or a delusional state caused by withdrawal. I read a lot about drugs used to treat malaria in the forties and about the symptoms of depression. I tried to believe this plausible explanation.

During the search, my brother and I would meet every once in a while for steak and red wine and talk about the findings, checking them against what we already knew. Mike was not as directly involved in the search as I was but he was supportive, and often came up with ideas. He found information on Lariam, a drug for travellers to prevent malaria. Lariam was now the subject of class actions because it caused severe psychological symptoms, including suicide, although rarely. But the drug had been used only since 1985 and the longest term effect reported was six months after it was taken. Even if some early form of the drug had been given to the military in the 1940s, it seemed unlikely the effects would linger for three-and-a-half years. Still, what we were learning was interesting.

But nothing fit perfectly, particularly as I got to know my father through his letters. He was serious, idealistic and ambitious but also conscientious and responsible. There was no suggestion that he was depressed. In all the letters, personnel files from the RCAF and RAF, there was no record of a major illness. His medical check-ups in the military and at discharge in 1945, a year and a half after his return from India, were unremarkable. He signed a witnessed declaration on discharge in November 1945 which required him to list all serious illnesses contracted during the war. The only one he named was amoebic dysentery and he reported that recent stool samples had been negative. Nothing in the autopsy suggested deterioration from a lingering illness. He took a course in the treatment of malaria when he was in India. He continued those studies after the war in a special course on tropical diseases in Washington. If he had had the disease, it seemed to me he would, at some point, have mentioned it to someone in the correspondence.

The remarks of senior officers on his war record were positive.

Very conscientious keen and efficient M.O. *who has left no stone unturned to maintain good health among all ranks. His efficiency has been reflected by the standard achieved despite overcrowded barracks conditions. A fine example in the officers mess and on the station as a whole.* (June 6, 1941)

A zealous hard working medical officer with exceptional ability in the duties on which he was engaged. No effort was too much for S/L Riley and he was a great loss to my wing when he was posted. (March 23, 1944)

Capable doctor with four years service experience. Consider an excellent service medical officer. (August 9, 1944)

At the end of January, 1944, as Bill Riley headed home to get married in Winnipeg, the Secretary of the Department of National Defence for Air in Ottawa received a note from the head of the RCAF Overseas. The letter revealed a favorable, unsolicited report from D'Arcy Power, Head of the Air Command in South East Asia on S/L Riley's tour of duty in India.

> *Dear Hunter,*
>
> *I don't know whether S/Ldr. H.W. Riley, RCAF has gone to U.K. or direct to Canada but I should like to draw the attention of either yourself or the Canadian authorities to the extremely good work he has done in India first as an M.O. with No. 413 Squadron, RCAF and for the past 8 months as SMO of 172 Wing, RAF. He is thoroughly reliable, very keen and a first rate mixer; I have never heard anything but the most glowing accounts of his work from everyone with whom he has come in contact. The real reason for writing the above is that I hope you will see that he gets a really good job when he returns either to you or to Canada. I am most sorry to lose him from this Command.*

I reviewed the evidence after he returned to Canada. He got top marks in the course in Washington, held responsible jobs in medicine in Calgary and back in Winnipeg and was invited into one of the most prestigious clinics in the city to set up practice as an internist. It was not sounding like he was ill or depressed. If he had an incurable disease, would he not have thought about insurance to support his family? Few policies paid on suicide in those days. It was not making sense to my journalistic/legal brain. Something was always missing.

But I was developing a picture of the father I had never known. The adjective that kept recurring was "different." My mother in her diary: *Bill is not like other boys, I have never been sure of his love.* One remark my mother made to me kept coming back. "We were so inexperienced," she told me in one of her few references to sex. I had never heard of other women in his life. Spending his last night before leaving London for Ceylon in 1942 talking with an old family friend seemed perfectly in character. All the other war memoirs I read made constant references to women, or lack of women, in the service and made much of any leave when the men could go and find women. These were men in the prime of their lives.

When I asked other people about him, the answer was that he was "different from the other Rileys." What was different? It's true that most of the cousins went into engineering or business and he was in medicine. But it was more than that. Many of them rowed and hunted while, in military application forms, Bill listed individual sports: golf, badminton, tennis. Never team sports. For hobbies he put "literature." And he wrote poetry. He seemed to have a vulnerability, a sensitivity that people describing him tried to put into words. "You're not like your father," Bill's cousin told Mike. "He wasn't nearly so, so…" He paused, searching for the word. "Robust," he finally finished.

One of the difficult things about discovering the suicide of a parent a long time after the death is readjusting one's view of the world. The delayed news certainly, in my case, eroded trust. If my family was not truthful about this important thing, what else did they leave out? What more were they hiding? Why were they so afraid of the truth? I also wondered, if everyone else knew, how did it affect others' view of me? Did they feel sorry for me? It changed my view of my mother and, instead of always looking to her for support, I began to feel empathy for her. How did she survive in the silence and guilt after his death, I wondered.

In this next phase of my search, I looked for anybody who might still be alive who could talk to me about him. By now, approaching the story as a journalist, I was more persistent with my questions than I had been when I was younger. I wasn't as inclined to accept that people knew nothing. The archivist at the Winnipeg Clinic told me he knew of only two doctors who had practiced at the Clinic during those years who were still alive and in Winnipeg. I found one of them: an obstetrician who had been there in 1945. He was by then 92. He remembered Bill Riley as a tall, slender man, in uniform the first time they met. "Your father was a quiet person, not unfriendly but not boisterous. I remember when he spoke to you he would sometimes look away as if he were seeing something way in the distance. There wasn't anything rude about this, just something I remember." He said doctors at the Clinic were shocked by his sudden suicide and a story circulated that he had had "an incurable disease." He said he hoped that bit of news might give me some comfort. I tried out some of the other stories on him. He said Bill Riley showed no signs of depression. He felt almost sure he would have noticed if Bill had been depressed. He also said my father had no symptoms of being on drugs or of heavy drinking.

The wife of another surgeon who practiced at the clinic with my father repeated the "incurable disease" rumor. My godmother Marge Johnston and her husband had seen a lot of my mother and father in those two years after they returned to Winnipeg. She said Bill was good company and lots of fun. The weekend before his last one at Keewatin, our family had visited the Johnston's at their cottage at Matlock and we had been invited again. "At the last minute, Sheila called to say they couldn't come, that they had to go to Keewatin. She sounded a little upset." Marge said the O'Gradys wanted to talk to them about possibly buying the cottage at Keewatin. There seemed to be some urgency that the discussion take place that weekend. Marge also said she had always thought that, if they had just come to Matlock, this terrible thing would never have happened.

One evening, at a dinner party, I was reminded of the slipperiness of oral history. My aunt Lois was visiting from Montreal and I was seated next to her childhood friend Marg Green. When I mentioned that I was writing a book about my father, she looked a little startled and offered the fact that she was one of the last people to see him alive. Until then, I had accepted Larry's version of that last evening in August 1947: that the three people in the car that night were Larry, my grandfather O'Grady and Bill. Marg Green corrected that version. She said she was the third person in the car and that my grandfather was not there. She was working at the Winnipeg Clinic at the time and she remembered vividly the incessant loudspeaker voice that Monday morning: "Calling Dr. Riley. Calling Dr. Riley."

"I remember the other doctors wondering where he was that day and I finally interrupted them to tell them that I had seen him the night before. It wasn't till the next day that I learned what had happened."

Other than showing the fallibility of long-term memory, the change in the story didn't make much difference to the mystery other than giving me another person to ask about my Dad. Marg Green, like Uncle Larry, couldn't remember anything out of the ordinary about the trip in from Keewatin that night. "Larry was driving and your Dad sat in the back seat. He didn't say much but he was a quiet, pensive person and his silence didn't seem anything unusual for him."

She had also heard that he had malaria during the war and had accepted that as an explanation when she heard the shocking news that he had killed himself.

I continued looking for people who had known my father. E-mail had made this inquiry easier than it would have been earlier but now most of the key people I should have been contacting were dead. I reviewed the newspaper clipping from the wedding in 1944 and the funeral in 1947. Buzz B., described as "Squadron Leader Lennox B." was best man at the wedding and ushers were Dr. Jack Lederman and Sanford Riley, "cousin of the bridegroom." Buzz B. was now dead and we had already asked him what he knew. Both Jack Lederman and Sanford Riley died of cancer as young men. Pallbearers at my father's funeral were Dr. Lennox B., Dr. John Lederman, C. S. Riley Jr., Brian Dickson and Larry O'Grady. They were all gone.

I then turned to my own friends from high school to ask what they had known about my father. One friend remembered hearing her parents refer to my father as "the Riley who committed suicide." Most knew he had killed himself and wondered, at the time, why I didn't know. But no one had wanted to be the first to tell me. My roommate in boarding school remembers asking from the other bed in the dark how my father died and the darkness hid her shock when I truthfully said I didn't know.

One of my friends, now living in Sydney, Australia, suggested I write her aunt who had grown up on South Drive, near the Rileys. The aunt, now in Rochester, New York, had some memories of my grandparents.

I thought your grandparents somewhat daunting. Was it because I was afraid they might catch us filching fruit from the

> *raspberry patch behind their house? They once offered me a ride*
> *when I was walking home from kindergarten along Point Road,*
> *which I refused because I was afraid of them.*

But she had been younger than my father and moved away from Winnipeg before the war. She suggested a couple of other names of people who might help. I became busy with other things and forgot about them.

Then one afternoon I got an e-mail from Montreal with the subject heading, *Re: Rileys on South Drive*. The writer said he also had lived on South Drive and my friend's aunt had told him I was looking for stories about my father. He ended his amusing and lively memories of my father with this paragraph:

> *I remember also going with him several times to listen to music*
> *at the flat of Dr. Lennox (Buzz) B., an older Zete (Zeta Psi,*
> *Bill's university fraternity), and a brilliant physician. It never*
> *struck me that all the other guests at those pleasant evenings*
> *were male. Buzz B. was a closet gay and in those days of course*
> *he had to stay in the closet. Those musical evenings were his*
> *way, poor fellow, of looking for possible partners.*

I sat stunned for awhile. I had never known Buzz B. was gay. No one had ever told me this. It had taken a complete stranger, far from the Winnipeg he grew up in, to mention this fact casually in a memory of my father. At first it was just interesting but, for days later, I couldn't stop thinking about those musical evenings. Why was my father going to them and why was he taking a younger neighbor from South Drive?

More pieces started to fall into place. My father was often described as "different," sometimes a code word for what is not said. I know what it is to feel different, to feel it in your bones, to smell it at every social event and family gathering, to be the one who doesn't fit in the family picture. But my struggle was different because I live in a different time. I had to come to terms with my sexual orientation in a time when it was at least possible to contemplate, in a society beginning to accept gay couples. I thought about my parents' era. I couldn't imagine the terror and self-loathing that would come from the belief that your feelings are truly wrong, condemned by society, the law, religion, the medical profession and, certainly, your own family. Discovery in those days, in that society, would certainly mean losing everything you had worked for and loved in the world.

I thought back to the 1930s and '40s when my parents were growing up. I thought about the pressures to conform, about the expectations and duties that weighed so heavily. I thought about the Riley family in Winnipeg and the conservatism of that social group. I thought about the war as a diversion from the expectations and about the shame of being different, about taboos and secrets. And about laws against some kinds of love and a medical profession that said people who loved that way were mentally ill. I imagined the one thing Bill Riley could not admit to anyone, especially to his family and to his wife. He left no note, this man who wrote so much about his thoughts during his life.

My father's childhood friend speculated on what it might have been like in that other time that he knew better than I did.

> *Is it possible that your father had discovered that he was fundamentally gay? But there he was with a wife and growing family and in post-war Winnipeg of all places. Nor was he in the same position as B., who obviously had come to terms with his own sexual orientation at an early age and had learned how to operate in that suffocating Winnipeg milieu. What, then, was he to do? If one adds another ingredient, that his entire outlook and value system—except for his lately discovered homosexuality—was probably deeply conservative, it is not difficult to see that he may have felt he had come to an absolute dead end.*

CHAPTER 16

COLOURED SPECS

The revelation about Dr. B. pushed my search in a new direction. Instead of concentrating on the war years, I turned to what I could find out about my father's earlier life. With the new information about his friend Buzz, I began to look back on my father's life with new openness, to explore all possibilities, and to look for clues I might not have noticed before. I re-read the letters from childhood and the early school years. I wanted to understand the family and community around my father, to soak up that era and that social class.

Bill Riley was born in Winnipeg in 1916, the year conscription was adopted in England and just before America's entry into World War I. On September 1, 1917, Aunty Anne wrote her sister-in-law Ivy Riley from London where she had just learned of the death of her husband Will Collum. He had died in battle in France and had just been buried by the military with no family present at Noeux les Mines, south of Bethune. At the end of her outpouring of grief and loneliness, Aunty Anne wrote *my love to the dear little lad*, a greeting to Bill Riley, the nephew she had not yet met. Anne Collum never married again but, having inherited money from her father, a pioneer Winnipeg grain merchant, became a philanthropist to city cultural organizations, especially the Royal Winnipeg Ballet. She remained close to the Riley family, especially Bill and his younger sister Eleanor.

On November 29, 1923, R. T. Riley wrote a letter to his seven-year-old grandson:

> *Dear Billy,*
>
> *I was very much surprised to get your letter in the mail this morning and I was very proud to see what a nice letter you*

could write. If I was your teacher, I would give you 100 marks in writing and composition each but instead of that I will have to ask Santa Claus to be very good to you and I will tell him what a nice grandson I have. I am glad to hear that you are taking gymnastics because then you will be such a big boy and able to take care of your little sister,

Your loving Grandfather, R. T. Riley.

The letter is typed on The Northern Trusts Company stationary with the signature handwritten in thick pencil.

R. T. Riley was by then a well-known western Canadian businessman, a director of the Royal Bank and the Canadian National Railway. Having emigrated from England by himself in 1873 at age of twenty-two, he started working on farms in Ontario and soon got a job with Sanford and Company, a Hamilton clothing firm. In 1881, Sanford sent him to Winnipeg. A bumper prairie crop in 1887 fuelled a boom in the West and Winnipeg began to take shape with paved streets and sewer and water. R. T. Riley saw the need for financial and insurance institutions based in the West. He set up the Canadian Fire Assurance Company, followed by the Northern Trusts and Canadian Indemnity. He was one of the founders of the Great-West Life Assurance Company and proud to hold insurance policy "number one." He served on the Winnipeg General Hospital board and was a member of the Methodist, later United, Church. As one of the founders of Winnipeg's commercial elite, he was also a member and later president of the Winnipeg Board of Trade and twice served on city council in 1887-88 and 1907-08. He was Conservative in politics and conservative in values.

With his first wife Harriet Murgatroyd, R. T. had nine children, seven sons and two daughters. John Herbert, Bill's father, was the eighth child. Herb, my grandfather, joined Northern Trusts and was its general manager until it was sold in the 1950s to Montreal Trust. The other Riley sons became well known in Winnipeg for their own various business ventures and the continuation and success of R. T.'s financial empire.

This was the family setting into which Billy Riley was born. Herb, instead of settling in the more established parts of central Winnipeg, chose to build a house on South Drive in Fort Garry, an undeveloped area south of the city. He and his young wife Ivy moved there shortly after they were married in 1910 and made Fort Garry their home. Herb was reeve of the Fort Garry Municipality and Riley Crescent was named after him.

The Rileys were a large and close family. By the time R. T. died in 1944 at age ninety-three, he had twenty-two grandchildren and twenty-four great-grandchildren. As one of the many grandchildren, Bill went to his grandfather's on Westgate for tea on Sunday afternoons. He grew up in a family where the underlying motto was "from those to whom much is given, much is required." They were competitive in sports, especially rowing, put a high value on achievement, were not given to showing emotion and, were dedicated to community and family.

Because there were no suitable schools in Fort Garry, Billy Riley was driven everyday into central Winnipeg to a school for the children of the elite. On "Fort Rouge Preparatory School" letterhead, he wrote to his father:

> Dear Daddy,
>
> I started school yesterday. I am now in Grade Six. Mrs. P. is still my teacher. This morning we began to learn square root...Yesterday was the Dominion election and the Liberals got in.
>
> Love, Billy.

My guess is that the election results were significant to a seven-year-old because he knew the family would have preferred the Conservatives.

In March of 1930, Aunty Anne took fourteen-year-old Billy on a trip to California. Aunty Anne wrote Ivy on the fifteenth anniversary of her marriage to Will Collum that she had dreamed about Will the night before. Billy came to her door early with some lovely sweet peas. Anne said she and Billy had gone to see Aimee McPherson (a preacher) but she made him promise to wait until he got home to tell them about it.

Billy wrote to his mother from Los Angeles that the desert was not too hot and that he had bought a pair of coloured specs. He wrote his sister, beginning:

> *Dear Eleanore—Please excuse the spelling of your name but the 'e' jumped on before I could stop it...yesterday I went twice to church so you can see I am not forming any bad habits. In the morning the minister preached for an hour and a half about nothing and in the evening there was a lady minister and whatever you did the people around you would say "God Bless you" and "the Lord be with you". I soon got the hang of it and called out "amen" every 2 minutes during the prayers and sermon. When they sang "My country tis of thee" I nearly drowned them out with "God save the King". The lady minister wore a blond wig.*

Bill went to Kelvin high school until 1932 when, at age sixteen, he was sent to boarding school at Ridley College in St. Catherines, Ontario where he stayed for two years, graduating in 1934. I know from my mother that he hated Ridley mostly because the expectation was that the boys participate in all sports, especially rowing and football, and he was more interested in reading. Because of all the recent exposure of sexual abuse in boys' schools, I thought I should see what I could find about his Ridley days. I only found one of his letters home from those two years. Written in March of 1933, the letter told his parents a story which *may seem funny to you but I am just beginning to get a little of its humour.* It was a long story about how one of the schoolmasters made him and two friends, as punishment for breaking rules, sing a solo in front of the whole school.

> *Came the appointed time, one hundred and fifty boys and masters were gathered in the assembly hall for singing. The three of us got through our verses somehow but I don't know how. I have never been so utterly embarrassed and taken by surprise as I was then. I hope I never again draw such a lemon because Ed and I had done nothing all week but tease Ross about his solo. Everyone in the hall just roared when we*

finished and did we feel cheap because, as you can imagine, we were awful. I don't think that Ed and I will be able to hold our heads up all term after that demonstration. I thought this incident might interest you.

Your affectionate son, Bill.

In the summers of 1934 and 1935, Bill and his friend Ed Sellers went to Europe. Bill wrote from London that he had bought a geared bike for thirty shillings which would have cost seven pounds new. They biked through the English countryside and into Scotland. Many years later, when I wrote to Ed's sister (married to Supreme Court Chief Justice Brian Dickson) to ask for her memories of my father, she produced an image of that trip.

Dear Susan,

I am very sorry to tell you that I can't add anything to what you already know about your father's death. Both your parents were close friends of ours and we were shocked and saddened to hear of his death. He was a very good friend of my brother Edward through Ridley, Medical School and their wonderful bike trips through Europe. There is one picture especially I remember somewhere in France with their bikes and long loaves of bread sticking out of their knapsacks—I wish I had it for you!

The daughter of old friends of my Riley grandparents added some memories from her days growing up with my father. *Yes, I knew your father and a fine clever person he was—always a bit shy but lots of fun.* She remembered when they started to go to dances at the Country Club. *On several occasions Billy and I were paired together—though he was a bit shy—we managed to enjoy the parties.* They both went away to boarding school and didn't see much of each other for many years.

Our paths didn't cross—thus I was very shocked to hear of his death. The war years took a heavy toll on doctors like your father...Today is October 10, 2002 which means I am 85

*and, as you can see, my writing is not getting any better. So I
hope this is OK.*

When I phoned to thank her for her help, she added another image. She
said that when they would go to a dance together he would be very polite
and have the first dance with her and also knew enough that he should
have the last dance with his date. But, in between, she said he would
be found wandering about the grounds outside, waiting for the dance
to end.

My father's childhood friend in Montreal, Alan A., supplied
further vignettes from the time of his growing up in Fort Garry. His first
memory of my father was when Bill was a medical student and he was a
freshman at the University of Manitoba. They were sitting cross-legged
on the floor in the sunroom at 749 South Drive with a fedora in front
of them.

> *Bill had filled his hat with slips of paper. On one side of each slip
> he had written a medical term and on the other side the correct
> answer. My role was to pick out a slip at random, read the
> question and wait for his answer. If he got it right, I set that slip
> aside; if wrong, it went back into the hat. We did this until the
> hat was empty and then started all over. By the time we were
> finished, I felt myself a complete master of human anatomy.*

> *During my freshman year I had resisted successfully the
> pressure to join a fraternity. In the fall of my sophomore year,
> however, I found myself under the influence of your father's
> strong persuasion. I was virtually innocent of liquor and I fear
> that I drank much beyond my limit and, with the help of your
> father's persuasive rhetoric, promised to join Zeta Psi. In the
> early hours he dropped me off at my house. I staggered up to
> my bedroom and at the top of the stairs struck my forehead a
> fearful blow on the newel post. Next morning, Mother was not
> amused to find a towel covered with blood and a huge wound
> on my forehead. All of which illustrates, perhaps, the avuncular
> role your father played in my life at that time.*

A younger cousin remembered Bill at his Zete initiation. The ritual involved blindfolding the new recruits and driving them all over the place until they were confused and worn out. He was fed up with the whole thing when they brought some of the "elders" into the room. "I only recognized one voice and it was my older cousin Bill. He told me seriously about the friends he made and how important the fraternity was in his life. I'll never forget that."

I know very little about his life as a doctor. But my mother kept a little book on her shelf called *Glowing Hearts*, the story of the pioneering days in Canada of a United Church Minister named Reverend Jim Shaver. I found inside the book a sympathy note to my mother dated September, 1947. It provided a little picture of my father as a physician.

Dear Mrs. Riley,

I am just one of your husband's patients…Your husband, to us, was much more than a physician. He was a personal friend who inspired love and confidence in a peculiar way. His attitude, not only to me but to my family, when all bothered him for "inside information" was so kindly and so understanding we shall always look on him as a personal friend…Here I am, an old man of three score and ten saved for perhaps a few more years by the skill and kindness of the young man who is taken… We can only pray that the richness of his short life may be a memory of comfort to you and serve as an inspiration to your little ones as they grow old enough to understand what you will have to tell them about their father…

He ended with a P.S.

During my darkest days when your husband told Mrs. Shaver the worst, she remarked, "But I believe in miracles," and he replied, "So do I." JMS.

CHAPTER 17

DR. B

I was now much more interested in Buzz B. and tried to find out anything I could about his life and, because he was a prominent doctor in Winnipeg, much of his story was public. He was eleven years older than Bill Riley and grew up in a very different environment from South Drive. I only met Buzz B. once and I now realize it must have been shortly before he died in 1973. He had been ill for some time with complications from diabetes and died at age 69. His friends report that he was a heavy drinker.

His close friends suspected he was gay, but he never talked to them about that and they did not press. Even his niece and nephew did not know he was gay until after he died. He had several women friends— some were wives of close friends—who liked to accompany him to social events because he was an entertaining and handsome partner. He had a lively social life and hung around with a crowd in the exclusive area of central Winnipeg where he lived. The group included the editor of the *Winnipeg Free Press*, the head of the Hudson's Bay Company and other prominent citizens, all with wives.

A friend of Dr. B.'s helped me understand what may have happened the only time I met him with my brother in the early seventies. He said that, although he and Buzz were good friends, they never talked about his homosexuality. Some of the doctors knew Dr. B. was gay but he never spoke about it. How did you know, I asked, if no one ever talked to him about it? "Well, it was obvious to us," he answered. "He would have these parties and one of the male guests would always be the last to leave." I asked if he had ever had a steady partner. "Oh no, not in those days. It would have been impossible in his position." He added that later in his life he probably had a partner in New York. "Buzz went to New

York a lot and always for a short period of time, usually a weekend. I always assumed there was someone there."

He said he had often observed B. neatly slide the topic in another direction when the subject of homosexuality came up. "He was so intelligent that most people did not even notice as they were carefully manipulated into another area of conversation."

"It was the worst thing you could say about someone in those days," said one of the doctor's wives who remembered that era. She tried to describe to me the society in Winnipeg. "I graduated from nursing and got married in the same June. I never worked as a nurse. The doctor's wife was not expected to work. Even though my husband often did not collect his bills and we lived on very little, it was not considered right for a doctor to have a working wife." She explained that some of the wives knew that Buzz B. was gay but no one would have dared talk about it because they liked and admired him.

B.'s career would have been finished if anyone had known the truth for sure. And Dr. B. had a distinguished career, becoming Dean of Medicine of the new Manitoba Medical College. It was a prestigious position and B. deserved it as a brilliant physician and dedicated teacher. But the appointment also had its politics and others campaigned for the job. No one openly gay would have been a candidate.

I looked back on our evening with Buzz B.. Mike had called him to ask for the meeting saying we wanted to talk to him about our father Bill Riley and his suicide. He agreed and invited us to his place. He lived in No. 2 on the main floor of an old red brick mansion and his suite was elegantly furnished and spacious. I later learned that the house, built by a prominent Winnipeg family, was by that time divided into suites, all of which were occupied by single men. Dr. B. greeted us politely that evening and offered us a drink, but he did not have much to say about our father's suicide. He talked vaguely of speculation about drugs and his suggestion to my mother after one party that she "do something about Bill." That was all. He expertly turned the conversation to other things and Mike and I were both inexperienced enough to listen politely and not press further. I had no idea he was gay and neither did Mike. I was a journalist working at one of the Winnipeg dailies at the time and B. wanted to talk about a memoir he had written on growing up at Fox Lake, a remote area where his father had built a fishing and hunting lodge.

I was not interested then but I have since read *Fox Lake*, the memoir he ultimately wrote, to try to understand more about him and the role he may have played in my father's life. B. grew up in a slightly eccentric household surrounded by scientists, his father's intellectually curious colleagues. His father was the first public health official in the province of Manitoba and did pioneering work in disease control. He died at age sixty from a deadly infection he caught trying to nurture a culture to protect the public from an infectious disease outbreak. A Winnipeg high school was named after him.

Buzz B. was only nineteen when his father died in 1923 but he was greatly influenced by him, both as a scientist and as a person. While Buzz, the only son, was still very young, Dr. B. Senior accepted the job as provincial bacteriologist and set up a lab in a one-story building on Kate St. on the grounds of the old Medical College. It was there that he began his tradition of welcoming doctors, teachers and anyone connected with medicine to sit on lab stools and chat about clinical problems or whatever was on their minds.

Buzz recalls in the memoir of his father written in 1970 that he was allowed to visit the lab and its animals on Sunday mornings. He was exposed to some great minds during his childhood and not all were doctors. His father loved music and the theatre and his children, Buzz and his sister, went to plays at the Walker Theatre and were surrounded by books and records from their earliest days.

In the Fox Lake memoir, Buzz writes about the influence of summers at that retreat. A group of doctors, including his father, pooled their funds and bought a property on the south shore of the remote lake and built a log clubhouse, naming it after the silver trout plentiful in the lake. Buzz looked back to his childhood and recognized that much of who he was came from those summers at Fox Lake and the teachings of his father. He taught young Buzz about the plants and animals in the area and instilled in him the joy of gaining knowledge by the touch and feel of experience. It was what made him an unusual diagnostician later in life, knowing that only so much could be learned in books. As a child, he learned to observe animals in their natural habitat and to believe what he saw and not what he read about. Buzz wrote warmly about those days and about the father he loved and lost at an early age.

The 1928 University of Manitoba yearbook says "Buzz" is one of the select few who *do many things and do them well*. Even then, as he graduated in medicine, he was known as a *strong leader and executive, good student and after-dinner speaker 'par excellence'*. He had won a scholarship and was author of "Sparks from the Daily Grind", a column in the medical school paper. He also expressed scorn for the yearbook write-up, calling it a *platitudinous blurb*.

When Buzz himself died, also at a young age, a friend wrote a tribute.

> *His clinical acumen was legendary. The speed and ease with which he reached a difficult diagnosis resembled a conjurer's trick. His powers of observation were acute and he could assemble apparently unrelated signs to provide an integrated interpretation of the case... At no time was this more evident than on his Sunday morning rounds when he would gather a group of junior medical students and walk the medical wards of the General Hospital. Students would be asked to observe a patient and they would look and look. Finally, under his gentle prodding, they saw...Many students can recall evenings at his home where there were always amusing tales and good music, food and drink.*

All this was very likely true, as far as it went. But it avoided a central truth about the life of Buzz B., just as important as the awards and professional successes. The tributes never talked about who and how he loved. There are those who will say that is none of anyone else's business. But secrets do have a way of becoming destructive and damaging when they affect the lives of others. The people who talked to me about that society and that time said they were silent about any hint of homosexuality out of respect for people they otherwise liked. But they didn't see that the silence became damaging in people's lives when it became a cover-up and when the stakes of maintaining the secrets were high.

Buzz B. was my father's mentor in medicine. When Bill graduated in 1939, he was accepted as a resident and teaching fellow in internal medicine under the guidance of Buzz B.. No doubt they spent many Sunday morning rounds together, B. teaching the subtleties of clinical diagnosis. When Bill returned from the Far East, B. was best man at his and Sheila's wedding in March 1944. When Bill was discharged from the service in 1945, with B.'s help, he joined a group of other internists at the Winnipeg Clinic. Both attended the clinical meetings in the evenings where the clinic doctors discussed interesting cases. And finally, Buzz B. was a pallbearer at Bill's funeral in August 1947.

CHAPTER 18

BLACKMAIL

I was a little early for my brunch date so I walked through the fresh snow past the Ritz Carlton and up the mountain on Cote des Neiges in the heart of English Montreal. Black footprints on the wet pavement marked my path. The streets of Westmount brought back vivid memories of the late sixties when I came here to work for the *Gazette*, just out of journalism school. Those were exciting days in Montreal and in journalism. The Front de Liberation de Quebec kidnapped the Quebec Justice Minister and Prime Minister Trudeau passed the War Measures Act. "Just watch me," he said to the journalists who questioned his authority. It was another time in Canada and in my life. I was just twenty-two and still unaware of my father's suicide and my mother's Alzheimer's.

Now, I turned into the courtyard leading to the townhouse. My father's childhood friend from Fort Garry, Alan A., now eighty-four, was tall and handsome with thick white hair and a hearing aid. We immediately relaxed around the dining table with baguette, lox, cream cheese and, very soon, a bottle of chilled Chablis. He talked about growing up in Winnipeg and the stifling atmosphere that he longed to escape as a young man. He talked about gay friends he had in those days and how difficult it was for them being in the closet. He remembered one friend who, before he was able to come out, had some violent encounters searching for men in dangerous places. One night he returned to the house they shared, bloodied with a broken arm. He could not remember where he had been.

He said gay men looking for partners in the 1940s often found them in all male clubs or organizations. Fraternities were a source of possible partners. There was a certain meeting of the eyes which signaled interest and, if it was not returned, could be ignored by both participants. And denied, if necessary. He remembered Winnipeg in those days as a particularly conservative place with little tolerance for difference. He himself left after his undergraduate degree and never went back except to visit family.

Then the conversation turned to Buzz B. and blackmail. When Buzz B. died in 1973, the executor of the estate discovered that a Winnipeg man had been extorting money from B. on threat of revealing that he was gay.

"Although they had been close to their uncle all his life, his niece and nephew had never known he was gay until after he died," he said. I e-mailed his niece in Ontario and his nephew in Montreal. The niece replied right away. *I loved my uncle but up to his death knew nothing about the fact that he was gay—can you believe??*" She said she knew nothing about blackmail. Finally the nephew replied. He had reviewed the correspondence in B.'s estate papers and found no mention of Bill Riley. *Rather the correspondence concerns a lawyer in Winnipeg, J. D., who often requested funds from my uncle.* The letters also mentioned a Dr. S. who, rumor had it, left his practice in Winnipeg after he was caught by police with an underage male. He suggested the College of Physicians and Surgeons might be able to help as he thought complaints were made about Dr. S. in the 1940s.

We were walking across the Burrard Street Bridge in Vancouver a few months later when I related this new information to a friend from journalism school days. She stopped in the middle of the bridge and turned and stared at me. "I think I know who the blackmailer is," she said. She recognized the name of the lawyer J. D. who had requested money from B.. She had known him as a child, the half brother of a friend. The friend was still living in Winnipeg. When I found her, she was eighty-eight and happy to talk about the old days. Orphaned as babies, she and her sister had been adopted by their aunt, married to an executive with one of the railways. They lived a grand life in a large house in one of Winnipeg's most prestigious neighborhoods. The wife hosted bridge games dressed in floor-length gowns and they had a private rail car for holidays. They raised the two orphans and then had three children of their own. One of the three studied law and joined a Winnipeg firm. His name was J. D.

"He was always the life of the party. When he walked in, the room came to life," she said. She didn't know then that he was an alcoholic but said he died of cirrhosis in 1981. Because he was fired from the law firm, she always wondered how he made a living. She confirmed that he was a good friend of Buzz B..

CHAPTER 19

SECRETS

I learned something about the Winnipeg social elite when I was sent to private school at Balmoral Hall in 1957. I was twelve and beginning Grade Seven. I didn't want to go, having just made friends in my new elementary school after my mother's remarriage. Probably because of my father's bad experience at Ridley, Sheila had not made Mike go when the Rileys wanted to send him away to Ridley, but she convinced me to try Balmoral, maybe because her own experience at private school had been good.

In the late forties and early fifties, the tuition at Balmoral was too high for middle class families emerging from ten years of depression. A new middle class would form in the post-war boom but many of the old families still had enough inherited wealth after the war to carry on the luxuries of their parents. They sent their daughters to private school not always to get a superior education but because the mothers had gone there themselves and, sometimes, their mothers' mothers. It was where you met the right kind of people and probably made the connections to marry the right kind of people, men your family would find acceptable. "There really weren't very many of us in those days," one of the women explained.

Today, I can laugh with old school friends about the dances at Balmoral where we sat, perspiration prickling under our arms, hoping a boy didn't try to talk to us because we would not know what to answer. One described her first day in a university class, after eleven years at a girls' school. A boy sat down beside her and attempted conversation. "What was I supposed to do? Nothing in my education had prepared me for this moment."

Our parents didn't talk about sex but there was lots of alcohol in their lives. Many of the parents were on their way to alcoholism by the time their children were in high school. The favourite social gathering in that class in the forties and fifties was the "cocktail party." Women wearing white starched aprons, holding alcoholic drinks on silver trays, glided among the guests. Scotch on the rocks was a favorite. A popular appetizer was "pigs in blankets," tiny sausages wrapped in pastry, so steaming hot they had to be held in a napkin. Most of the guests smoked and every side table held crystal ashtrays. After the party, they got in their cars and drove home for late dinners.

They belonged to the same clubs. In Winnipeg, leaders in business and politics gathered at the Manitoba Club. It was for men only and did not admit Jews. Neither did the St. Charles Country Club, the prestigious golf club for the Anglo Saxon elite, or the Winnipeg Winter Club, the sports complex. Most chose to live in the south end of the city, south of the CPR tracks and many didn't know anyone from the "North End," the area of the city where immigrants, largely Ukrainian before the war, settled.

When war was declared in 1939, Winnipeg was still run by the commercial elite, many of whom immigrated from Ontario and made their fortunes in business while the Prairie town grew through years of boom and bust. These men had built hardware stores, grain companies and, later, financial institutions, making Winnipeg the trading centre for a larger rural area. Their fortunes grew through business and real estate investment and it become important to protect wealth by controlling politics. The businessmen who ran the Board of Trade also ran Winnipeg. It was not until 1956 that Winnipeg elected a non Anglo Saxon mayor, Steve Juba.

The year after Steve Juba was elected, I was sent to Balmoral Hall. By then, I was somewhat of an outsider. I had not grown up in the same social set as my new classmates at the private school. I did not go to the Winter Club nor was I admitted into the side door reserved for women for Mothers Day dinners at the Manitoba Club. My grandparents had lived that life and been part of that social elite, but my father's death and my mother's remarriage meant I had spent five years in another social class, living in Norwood and going to public school. Now I was re-entering the world into which I had been born. My history always gave me a little distance.

My new classmates had horses. They skied in Banff on their Christmas holidays and lived in big houses on Wellington Crescent or on large properties outside of the city. I knew that my father grew up in that social class. When he went to medical school in the thirties there were still quotas on Jewish students. Only the war and need for doctors loosened up the quotas. My father's friends were now the fathers of my new friends at Balmoral. I know enough about that era to appreciate that being openly gay in Winnipeg in that social class in the forties and fifties was not possible. Affairs were possible, discreet ones. Even illegitimate children were possible and handled with finesse. Careful and secret liaisons between men were managed but, if they became public, careers were ruined, jobs were lost, divorces followed.

One newspaper story I found from 1946 reported that two young men had been convicted of extortion. They had demanded money from a Winnipeg man threatening to expose him for "an indecent act" they claimed to know he had committed. The man reported them to police and they were caught. I discovered that post-war Winnipeg was a place where being blackmailed for being gay was possible and, in fact, happened. But these circumstances were not easy to find out about because the act of blackmail was never talked about openly, or documented.

CHAPTER 20

DR. S

I continued my search for the Dr. S. mentioned in the letters to Buzz B.. I thought any confirmation of the rumors might tell me more about the Winnipeg-in-the-1940s society my parents lived in. And I wondered if his story would have anything to do with my father's death. As it turned out, the mysterious Dr. S. did have some strange connections to my family.

Many Winnipeggers knew vaguely of the story because it was a scandal at the time. One woman in her eighties remembered her father picking up the newspaper and exclaiming that "his" doctor had been convicted of a crime. People talked about a Dr. S. who had been driven out of practice in Winnipeg because he was gay. But no one knew exactly when or why and I couldn't find the newspaper stories without knowing the date. The date was important: the incident could only have something to do with my father's death if it had happened during the short time he was back in Winnipeg after the war, the period from 1945 until his death in 1947.

Wearing soft white gloves, I carefully turned the brittle pages of the bound yearly registers in the archival records of the Manitoba College of Physicians and Surgeons looking for Dr. S. The registrations were not alphabetical but filed by date. The work was slow and tedious but, at last, I found it. The registration of Dr. S. was dated 1937. But it was different from all the others. Scrawled across it in red ink were the words "erased from the register." He had been banned from the practice of medicine in the fall of 1946, the year before my father's death. And the story, as it unfolded, had other links to my family. It took me back to the end of the war.

My O'Grady grandparents had just bought a white clapboard house on Grosvenor Avenue in 1945. When Larry came back from overseas, he took the attic bedroom on the third floor and began to study for a Commerce degree. Even though my grandfather had lost his job, things were looking up for the family. Larry had survived the war and was getting an education, Lois had a job as a dietician and Sheila had married well and was producing grandchildren. My grandparents Elsie and Gerald had reason to be optimistic about their children's future.

Next door to the O'Grady's lived the S. family. Dr. S. Senior took his medical degree in Glasgow and arrived in Winnipeg as a young man. He set up a general practice on Sherbrook Street and married the daughter of a prominent city councillor. They had three sons. Two of them would grow up knowing they were gay. The eldest was Robert because he was the eldest son of the eldest son. Everyone called him Bobby. He was blond, blue-eyed and the apple of his father's eye. He was so charming people said he could have entertained the King and Queen. In the 1930s he studied medicine at the University of Manitoba, graduating in 1937, president of the medical fraternity Theta Kappa Psi and senior stick of the faculty. He and Buzz B. would become lovers.

Bobby had married before joining the Navy as a medical officer in 1940 and, then, home on leave in 1943, he told his wife he was gay. She immediately filed for divorce and Bobby moved back into the family home on Grosvenor, next to the one my grandparents bought after the war. The second S. son also followed his father into medicine, graduating the year after Bobby. After the war, he was hired as a surgeon at the Winnipeg Clinic. He and Buzz B. and my father attended the clinic's scientific meetings in the evenings during the summer of 1946. The third S. son knew he was gay when he was fourteen. But he was so traumatized by later events in his family that he was not able to pursue relationships with men until after his mother died at age ninety-five and he was in his late fifties.

One winter evening in 1946, the S. family threw a party at the house. Music, laughter, and the clink of ice in glasses spilled into the street in that conservative River Heights neighbourhood. When the police came to the door and asked for Bobby, his brother quickly agreed to go with him to the station before the other guests noticed. The two oldest brothers disappeared for a couple of hours but later returned to the party.

That part comes from sources who knew the S. family well. The rest of the story comes from newspaper clippings, college archives and a published report of the court proceedings. The *Winnipeg Free Press* reported in May, 1946 that Dr. S., age 33, had been tried in provincial court on two counts of contributing to the delinquency of juveniles. No conviction was entered by Justice F. A. E. Hamilton. A second story in the *Winnipeg Tribune* on May 8 was headlined "Winnipeg Doctor Sentenced to One Year." The *Tribune* reported that the attorney general of Manitoba had appealed the case to King's Bench. Mr. Justice Adamson sentenced Bobby S. to a year in jail.

I couldn't locate the original trial transcript. A few facts about what actually happened come from appeal records. In Juvenile court, after the prosecution put in its case, the defence moved for a dismissal. Judge Hamilton didn't grant the dismissal but continued with his own unorthodox solution.

> *Judge: Stand up please. (The accused did so.) You have heard the evidence. I am satisfied without any doubt whatever in my mind that you did interfere with this boy and I have to find you guilty on the evidence.*

Sensing his chance, Mr. McMurray, the defence lawyer, quickly seized the moment.

> *I presume Your Honour intends to dispose of the case now and we wish to plead guilty on the other case.*
>
> *Judge: Do you admit the age of the other boy?*
>
> *Mr. McMurray: Yes.*

Mr. McMurray then made a plea for clemency, pointing out that a conviction would mean loss of the licence to practice medicine and that the accused had served five-and-a-half years in the Navy under "terrible nervous strain."

> Mr. Elliott (the prosecutor): I leave the matter of sentence to
> Your Honour. I would not care to express an opinion on the
> sentence for this man."

Hamilton continued to address the accused:

> The Court has found you guilty. I know that must have been a
> very severe punishment to you...I am inclined to think the
> lesson you have had so far will make sure you don't repeat this
> kind of thing, so I don't intend to enter a conviction on the
> record at all...I know your previous record and I believe you
> can be a very successful citizen in this community...

He ended by assessing costs to be paid by the accused and with a
warning. *I don't need to tell you how careful you will have to be in the future.
You will have to be exceedingly careful.*

Adamson, on appeal by the Crown, rejected Hamilton's attempt
to salvage Dr. S.'s medical licence and sentenced him to a year in jail
on each count. Dr. S. appealed but the Court of Appeal upheld the
conviction and jail sentence.

Uncle Larry told me what he remembered of the incident. His
summer job at the time was driving Dr. S. senior, who couldn't drive
because he had been having seizures. Larry remembers his parents being
upset because the neighbours' son was going to jail. They told Larry that
Bobby was a homosexual.

The youngest S. son, twenty-two at the time, was told very little by
his parents. He remembers his mother standing with her back against
the radiator in the hallway, reading the *Free Press*. Suddenly, she called,
"Bobby, come with me." They left the room and the younger brother
knew it was serious.

The youngest S. brother was working at the Bank of Commerce
on the corner of Grosvenor and Stafford. Every Tuesday morning, the
bank would give him half a day off to visit his brother in jail. Each
Tuesday for six months beginning in July, the S. family would drive to
Headingley to see Bobby. He was released Christmas eve having served
half his term. From Christmas and through the summer of 1947, Bobby

was back living with his parents on Grosvenor. The family left on a driving trip to California later that fall, mostly to get out of Winnipeg. The younger brother remembers that Buzz B. was not around at all during the family crisis. He does however remember him later at the family cottage at Sandy Hook.

That day, searching in the Manitoba Archives, I found Bobby's original signed registration (1937) with the College of Physicians and Surgeons in the thick black binder along with Buzz B.'s (1928), his brother's (1938) and Bill Riley's (1939). The red writing across Bobby's explains:

> *Name erased from the Register by order of the council at the annual meeting October 1946.*

Underneath, also in red, it continues:

> *Restored to the register by the vote of the council at the annual meeting October 1947.*

The council minutes for the October 1946 meeting report that Dr. S. was erased from the register and quote section 43 of the *Medical Act* which said that a doctor convicted of anything would automatically lose his licence. The matter was not referred to the discipline committee because they said they had no discretion. They based their decision on newspaper reports and court records. The minutes of the annual meeting a year later report that, after an appeal from Dr. S., backed by several references, his licence was restored by a vote of eleven to two.

Years later, when he asked Buzz B. for money in a letter, the Winnipeg lawyer J. D. reported that Bobby was doing well practising medicine in London, England. But perhaps that was underestimating the effect of banishment from his home and family (he returned to Winnipeg to visit only once every three years). Bobby died in London at fifty-nine from what the coroner ruled an accidental overdose. When the youngest S. son returned from London after settling the estate, his mother asked him if Bobby was a homosexual. He confirmed what she already knew deep in her heart.

How Dr. S. got caught in Winnipeg that winter night in 1946 is unclear. The rumor in the gay community was that police were tipped off about Dr. S. and bugged a hotel room where he was caught in bed with a minor. Did someone blackmailing Bobby finally carry out the threat? Whatever the real story, Bobby almost got off without a criminal record. The first judge, Hamilton, simply did not enter a conviction and adjourned the hearing without a return date. How and why did the attorney general of Manitoba pursue the case and appeal? Bobby may have made enemies in high places in the Winnipeg establishment. His wife was the sister of the editor of one of the city's daily newspapers.

Because the story is true and over fifty years old, the incomplete facts will never provide all the answers. In the Criminal Code at the time, there was a section for Offences Against Morality. Buggery, "either with a human being or any other living creature," was punishable by life in prison. That was section 202. There was another section covering "any indecent act" and another for "gross indecency with another male person" which carried a punishment of five years in prison and a whipping. And, as an indication of the morals of the times, suicide was a crime as were unlawful carnal knowledge and abortion.

The Criminal Code offences would obviously have been more serious charges carrying more serious penalties but they were not laid in the case of Dr. S. The Crown proceeded with the much lesser charge under the *Juvenile Delinquents Act*. The act made liable the adults who in some way contribute to the delinquency of a child (defined as under 16). The punishment was a fine of up to $500.00 or a sentence of up to two years. Delinquency included violation of any law or being "guilty of sexual immorality or any similar form of vice." Bobby was convicted of contributing to the commitment of a delinquency by a child. Without all the court records, we don't know the whole story.

The importance of the case to me is what its notoriety would do to anyone in the medical profession at the time who was gay or suspected of being gay. The issue was complicated by the fact that the Bobby S. story could have been portrayed as being about molesting juveniles and not about being gay. That would be confusing to anyone wrestling with these issues in a time when little was known about them. There was never any suggestion later in life that Bobby was a pedophile and there was no evidence of force or violence in the single Winnipeg incident which sent him to jail. But the publicity around the event would certainly have been devastating in the gay community and would have had a chilling effect on the clandestine encounters necessary at the time. And it is inconceivable that my father would not have known the story of Bobby S. They had been in medical school together. The S. family lived next door to his wife's parents. His friend Buzz B. had been intimately involved with Bobby. His cousin's husband Jack Lederman was on the medical council at the time and my father was a colleague of one of the S. brothers at the Clinic.

The story is a part of the history of Winnipeg in the 1940s, an underground history seldom glimpsed. It's a window on a world no one in my parents' society admitted existed and families did their best to hide. And, if my father was struggling with his own sexuality at the time, the event would have been a clear sign that his situation was hopeless.

CHAPTER 21

A POEM, A BOOK, AND A LETTER

I have few things that belonged to my father. A small change purse contains his RCAF wings and his Zeta Psi fraternity pin, the one my mother wore on her slip through the war. A worn leather zippered briefcase holds a poem, a book and a letter, each giving me a small vivid snapshot of a bit of my father's life.

The poem evokes a picture of a young medical officer in Ceylon sitting at dusk under the palm trees searching for rhymes. This poem is in the form of a sheet of lined loose leaf, torn and frayed at the edges, on which he wrote in pencil a sonnet. On one side of the paper is the finished version with "Sheila" scrawled at the top. On the other side are his rough written notes with parts of lines scratched out and new ones written above, the rhythm marked above each word. He has written in the margin a series of rhymes he might try: "kin, din, pin, sin, bane, cane, fain, slain, vain, wane".

> Sheila
> I knew last night that you had thought of me,
> And raised your eyes a moment, with a look
> That flitted past the pages of your book
> To journey over countless leagues of sea;
> It was not sent in vain:
> For to my room a breeze stole quickly in
> And paused, as if to stay, and then did not.
> But I awoke at once, and thought your thought
> Which filled my soul with yearning from within.
> I did not sleep again.

With the book open in front of me, I see the young officer outside a book store in London hurriedly writing his name and turning the page before the ink is dry. It's a thin volume called *T. S. Eliot, Poems 1909 to 1925*, still in its paper jacket cover. "H. W. Riley" is written in black ink on the first page and the imprint of the wet ink is still on the facing jacket cover.

Finally, the letter helps me picture my father in his hotel room in old Delhi sitting up late one night thinking about Buzz B. after a day peering at slides under microscopes. It's an Air Mail Writing Tablet for sheets of paper advertised on the front as "Light As Air." The cover page and the cardboard backing are still intact but only two sheets are left. On them is a letter to Buzz B., never sent but saved in the writing tablet.

Delhi, March 16, 1943

Dear Buzz,

It's nearly two years since I have had anything but the merest snatches of news about you and I expect that is mutual. I am scribbling this to inform you that I still exist and have not degenerated into a pukka sahib, retaining my intellect at least to a certain extent.

My job since I saw you has been pretty much of a routine affair with the occasional flash of intense interest. The novelty of the first few months up north kept me keen and the keenness was renewed for a spell with the move to the East. The varnish has worn pretty thin by now however and sheer boredom has prompted me to look out for jobs that wouldn't have appealed very much a couple of years ago. As a matter of fact I am ready to tackle almost anything for a change provided I can get a little bit of action. Medicine's a dead issue until the war is over except from a very superficial standpoint. An RAF M.O. with any sort of clinical aspirations hasn't a hope in hell—the army runs all the hospitals. The best thing I could wrangle, and this only after a prolonged jeremiad, was a course in malariology. So here I am at the Malaria Institute of India turning into a malariologist so help me. As a matter of fact, the course is exceptionally good and after a long arid spell I am sopping up knowledge like a sponge. The essence of malariology is entomology and I am becoming so familiar with the anatomy of the various species of anopheles that I see their genital palmar hairs in my sleep. In fact I am becoming definitely abnormal.

The letter ends there and was never sent but kept throughout the war.

CHAPTER 22

PERCEIVED CRIMES

Throughout my journey, many people have expressed concern that the search would be too painful, that it would be futile, would not yield answers. I explained that more pain came from secrets, from the silence surrounding my father's death and his short life. So I have come to know two young people who fell in love in wartime Winnipeg and who both believed in the personal sacrifices that war demanded. I got to know my mother when she was young, a talented, hopeful woman who enjoyed her friends, her family and a busy life. I found my father, an idealistic, sensitive young doctor, a person I feel sure I would have liked. And, because I have learned something about his death, the fear of what I don't know is gone.

One of the last people I visited in my search was a doctor who was Manitoba's Chief Medical Examiner for over twenty years. From his long experience of investigating violent deaths, he suggested starting with a theory and trying, critically, to disprove it with facts. We began together with the death scene on Waverley Street, Tuesday August 26, 1947. Crumpled newspapers about the living room. Cokes and glasses on a table. These details were not in any official documents but reported by my aunt from what my mother had told her. The description of the body came from the autopsy. The report said the revolver was in his right hand (although Larry remembered it lying near his hand on the shower floor). The coroner stated cause of death as cerebral laceration and hemorrhage caused by the gunshot. The autopsy described the entry of the bullet at an angle on the right side of the forehead. The bullet was under the skin behind the left ear. The coroner has to establish identity, place of death, cause of death and manner or mode of death. There are five possibilities for the last category: natural, accidental, suicidal, homicidal or undetermined. The clues at the scene led the coroner to conclude death was suicidal. That is a judgment call.

First, the gun in the hand. The doctor said it's almost impossible to put a gun in the hand after death. If Bill had been left handed, he would not have been able to shoot himself the way the bullet had entered. I had been unable to determine whether my father was left or right handed. The doctor suggested that a picture of him with a cigarette might help. People generally smoke with the dominant hand. In the first pictures I examined, I was startled to see that my father was smoking with his left hand. In one picture, he was holding a drink with his left hand. However, I turned up several more pictures where he was smoking with his right hand. Nothing conclusive. Handwriting experts said they could not determine handedness.

The doctor immediately noted the needle mark on the inside of the left elbow. He pointed out that the autopsy showed my father had slight pneumonia in both lungs. "Your father would not have been feeling well. Both lungs were congested," he said. And he surmised that the needle mark meant my father had been to a doctor recently and had a blood sample taken. "I would have been looking for some kind of disease," he said. However, he could not find signs of illness, other than congested lungs. When I told him about the Far East, he looked for cerebral malaria, a disease that can cause psychosis many years later. But there was no sign of abnormal brain tissue. He said, in his experience, physicians either refuse to treat ailments in themselves or else they conclude that their symptoms are fatal. "There is no in-between with doctors. They either have nothing or they're going to die."

He said he always pays close attention to clues found around the body. The air force clothing in this case was important. "Did he lose a close friend in the war, perhaps a friend he thought he should have saved?" he asked. He said very few people leave suicide notes, the lack of explanation causing pain to those left behind. But they often leave clues. For example, a woman unhappy in marriage might take off her wedding ring. He said he always looks for signs of a past crime or a perceived crime. Sometimes people kill themselves when they have committed a crime and are about to be caught. When I told him about my father's friend Buzz B. being gay, he remained unimpressed. "What do you have but speculation? No connection."

But his interest returned when I told him that Buzz B. was paying for silence. Now, he said, I might have something. "Blackmail is a common cause of suicide," he said. He likened it to murder. He said even a suggestion that my father was gay in the 1940s would have ended his medical career. Even attending those "musical evenings" at the home of a gay friend was dangerous, enough to start rumors. But he added that his career would also have been ended by any suggestion of mental illness, including depression. And, he said, if my father had been having serious flashbacks related to the war, he would have been afraid to see a doctor as that also would have threatened his career. "He would have been hiding these things very well."

He explained why the coroner characterized the mode of death as "suicide while of unsound mind." This was a common phrase as suicide was a crime, defined in the coroner's office as "intentional termination of life." A person judged "of unsound mind" could not form intention. This often helped the family with insurance or with religious concerns. My father was buried in the cemetery at St. John's Anglican Cathedral and his funeral was in a church.

What about other clues at the scene? The military clothing, long after he had been discharged from the air force, did suggest a war connection. I had come up with nothing concrete from the war years. But trauma and post traumatic stress disorder (PTSD) were still possible. There was no sign of an incurable disease.

I visited a clinical psychologist considered an expert in PTSD. She described some of the symptoms, explained how one of the senses can trigger a strong flashback. She said smells are particularly powerful stimulants bringing back traumatic experiences. She said that relatives of victims of early wars were mystified by the behavior and didn't know what to make of it. Victims would go into a kind of trance when they had an attack. I had never heard from anyone about these kinds of symptoms in my father. But she also advised that my father would have been trying to hide any sign of mental "weakness" in the climate of the times, not wanting to jeopardize his medical career.

She was very interested in the military clothing he wore when he died and said that was an important clue. But she suggested something I had not thought of. She said that if my father was trying to hide a secret that would have been scandalous in those days—like homosexuality or blackmail or both—he might have used the military dress to divert attention from the real story. She added that the choice of clothing, with the sleeveless sweater on top, was not the act of a man proud of his military service but a kind of cry that he was "half a man."

I began my testing of theories. The Cokes and glasses did indicate someone else might have been there that night. The doors were locked from the inside. The visitor appeared to have been someone he knew. If he was being blackmailed by someone threatening complaints to the College of Physicians and Surgeons, he might feel helpless to defend himself, especially if he knew his friend Buzz B. was paying for silence. He would certainly have realized he could not hide an expense like that with his growing family and his in-laws' financial troubles. And he, unlike B., also had the added fear of hurting his wife and family.

Death would put an end to the fear and the shame. The air force revolver was perhaps hidden away, wrapped in newspaper in a trunk in the spare room. The old ammunition was with it, never used. The old military clothing packed away with the gun would seem easy to put on. They would suggest a connection with the war. And the basement shower would keep everything clean. It was only a theory but the facts did not disprove it.

As I was concluding this story, I received a letter from London, Ontario adding one more tiny piece to the puzzle. The writer was married to a doctor who had worked with my father at Deer Lodge Hospital just after the war. Her mother was supervisor of the officers' ward at the hospital and, she said, had been very fond of my father. *Several times he and Dr. Buzz B. went to our home for tea.*

She sent me a picture of my parents at a supper dance at the Fort Garry Hotel.

> *When my husband and I were to be married, I invited your mother and father to the wedding. They declined but sent us a*

beautiful blue Wedgwood vase which is a family treasure. Yes,
no one spoke about suicide in those days. I do not think we even
wrote to your mother afterwards.

I thought about this letter. It was confirmation of the taboo around suicide but also another mention of Buzz B. in connection with my father from someone who had no idea of my interest in their friendship.

CHAPTER 23

ENDINGS

I don't particularly remember anything about the last time I saw Marty. All the visits and letters now blend into a seamless friendship over fifteen years. I do remember being acutely aware during the last few times we said goodbye that it might be the last. I held her for a few seconds longer as we hugged and tried to soak up all the details of the house, the sounds and smells of that special place in my life. I think the last visit was when she was eighty-eight in 1997.

One Sunday in February of 2002, I answered the phone and a voice said it was Marty's friend from Columbia, Missouri. Marty had died two weeks earlier at age ninety-three. She had had a fall in the house. "We can't possibly keep Muffin," the friend explained quickly. "We were wondering if you would like her." I was shocked. "Well, we already have a large dog and two cats and we live in a condo. I don't think we could manage another dog," I said through my tears. "Oh," she said. "Well, I remembered that Marty had some Canadian friends and I just thought I would try."

After the phone call, Rhonda persuaded me we could take Muffin. The week before our neighbour Sharon had lost a four-year-old Springer Spaniel who died suddenly of a stomach ailment. Sharon said, "I have enough love in my heart for a ten-year-old Springer."

And so it was that we found ourselves driving south on I-29 with our Yellow Labrador, Missouri, curled up on the back seat. Before we picked up Muffin, we went to Marty's house to collect pictures of Marty and my mother at Camp Kamaji – evidence of a time long before Sheila`s Alzheimer-stricken fingers fumbled helplessly as she tried to button a blouse.

On the day before we left Columbia, we tried to get Muffin used to the idea of riding in the back of the Jeep in preparation for the long trip back to Canada. The first time she shivered violently and we had to turn back to her familiar ground. But gradually she got used to it and we thought she was ready for the trip. And early Sunday morning, she hopped up easily beside Missouri on the back seat and snuggled into a crocheted blanket that smelled of Marty. Missouri made himself very small by the window, giving Muffy virtually the whole back seat.

When we arrived in Winnipeg the next afternoon, our neighbour Sharon was waiting with tea and biscuits. We all anxiously watched Muffin for her reaction to the new surroundings and, suddenly, we realized to our horror that she had soiled the rug. "Oh, she must be nervous," said Sharon, calmly bending down and removing the waste with a Kleenex just as Marty would have done. We decided Muffin had found a new home only blocks away from where Elsie once walked "dear dog" in the park.

• • •

On March 17, 2003, I received an e-mail.

> To share with you this St. Patrick's Day: Your dad left Liverpool on this date 62 years ago from UK for destinations unknown, properly kitted with tropical gear. We were the first Canadian squadron to go o'seas from o'seas. Arrived Sri Lanka (Ceylon) in June.

It was from Gordon Ireland.

I visited Gordon and his wife Donna Mae a couple of weeks later in their retirement home on Vancouver Island.

"Has anyone ever told you that you look like your Dad?" He held up the newspaper photograph, yellowed and torn, beside my face. My father, in his mid-twenties, grinned under his air force hat. Gordon let the moment pass as I brushed my eyes with the back of my hand. "No one even talked to me about my father," I explained. He didn't hear about my father's death until long after the war, probably in 1950. "Did you hear what happened to Doc Riley?" asked one of his 413 buddies. Neither of them had any idea what had transpired.

When he returned to Winnipeg after the war in 1945, Gordon Ireland knew he would not stay. He was newly married with a baby son and working at the old Eaton's mail order. "There was nothing for me there. I had no education and it was a closed community to people like me. I had no connections and it seemed a dead end." He took his family to Whitehorse, re-enlisted in the RCAF and took overseas postings. When he retired from the forces at sixty he had another career in security in Calgary. When he retired a second time to Vancouver Island, he continued volunteer work. With his second wife Donna Mae, he made the trip to Sri Lanka for the dedication of the War Memorial to the twenty-one members of Squadron 413 who lost their lives in the defence of the island in 1942. Later, after Leonard Birchall's death, he organized a tribute to the "Savior of Ceylon" in Trenton, Ontario and I attended.

At the Irelands' home on Vancouver Island after our visit, Donna Mae took our picture in front of the tulips in the back yard and we said goodbye. Gordon promised to send me his own 413 insignia if he could find it. Back at our hotel, my daughter (who had been my driver for the trip) and I had just changed into white terry towel robes to have a steam before dinner. We realized we had no slippers and were a little embarrassed to have to put on running shoes with our robes. On our way to the pool, a man I recognized hurried toward us carrying a large package. Gordon Ireland handed me a framed painting of the Catalina that spotted the Japanese back in 1942, signed by Leonard Birchall, a momento of his trip to Sri Lanka in 1995. "I wanted you to have it," he said simply. He shook hands with my daughter and turned back as he headed to his car. "Nice running shoes," he said.

When I returned home, I had a letter, enclosing the 413 insignia, and some advice from Gordon Ireland.

> *With regards to your thoughts about his death and his early association with Buzz and including that he was his best man,*

I am more than inclined to agree. However if this were the case, the agony, mental anguish his marriage and two young children, profession, social status of families and overall high esteem in which he was received wherever his presence, would have been more than overwhelming in his decision making. Knowing the kind of person he was, kind and gentle, it would never be his intent to cause the hurt and disappointment that occurred. His pain was so intense he could not live with himself any longer. I wonder if his interest to pursue psychiatry was searching for answers to his personal dilemma whatever that may have been…However, Susan, remain positive, regardless of the circumstances, we are talking of someone who gave much of himself for others and was always held in high regard.

•   •   •

Because I worked downtown and lived in the south part of the city, I was not very often in the north end of Winnipeg. But, one summer afternoon, returning from a hearing in Selkirk, I realized I would be driving right past St. John's Cathedral cemetery where my father is buried. I had vague recollections of visiting his grave with my mother when Mike and I were very young. We played hide and seek among the gravestones and were probably a bit of a handful for her on those visits. On impulse, I turned off north Main Street to see if I could find anyone in the Cathedral who could tell me where his grave was.

The woman in the office consulted a map on the wall and pointed me to a row of graves, the second one in from the fence on the west side. I spotted a granite headstone down the row about two feet high with RILEY carved on both sides. A footstone embedded in the soil and surrounded by grass showed me where my father was buried. The other half of his plot was empty and grass covered. On the other side of the headstone, two footstones side by side identified the graves of my grandfather who died in 1960 and my grandmother who followed him there eight years later. They were buried just as they had lived, together.

Again, I was struck with that profound sadness. My father seemed so completely alone in death. Because my mother had remarried, she was not buried beside him in the plot that was presumably intended for his wife. The space beside him is empty and probably always will be. This 31-year-old man, so troubled in life, was buried alone. He lies on the other side of the stone from the parents who loved him and yet did not really know him. There is a barrier between them in death as there was in life.

It was only later that night that I noticed the date. August 24. I had visited my father's grave on the fifty-seventh anniversary of the day my father left my mother, my brother and me at Keewatin Beach. It seemed that day I had come full circle and that I certainly must have had a guide in this journey.

• • •

A photograph in one of the family albums is of my mother Sheila and my Riley grandparents, Herb and Ivy, on the front steps of the house on South Drive with the number 749 visible by the front door behind them. It was taken in 1948, shortly after the three of us moved in with the Rileys.

"If you enjoy the charm of a Tudor mansion here's your chance," the ad in the *Winnipeg Free Press* beckoned, fifty-five years later. The British couple selling 749 South Drive was happy to give a tour to the grandchildren of Herbert Riley, the man who built the house. My brother Mike and I were lost in our own thoughts as we walked through the house holding our earliest memories. We didn't talk much as we wandered from room to room except to answer the occasional question about what had changed since we had lived there in the early 1950s. An architect had remodelled the kitchen and taken out the back stairs. A picture window had been added to the dining room.

But it was still easy to imagine scenes in the house where my father grew up. I saw him in the sunroom with his friend drawing answers to medical questions out of a hat on the floor. I saw my mother's first visits to this house with her best friend from school, Eleanor Riley. Her diary told of a day when they skied in Fort Garry and returned to 749 for tea. *We sat in front of a fire in the living room. Their house is always so warm and welcoming*, she explained in her diary. I remember sitting in front of that red brick fireplace years later, perched on the arm of my grandfather's chair while he read Hurlbut's Bible stories to my brother and me.

Upstairs, across the front of the house was my grandparents' bedroom with the adjoining sunroom where they used to hide our Christmas presents. It was closed off in the winter and used for storage. One December, Mike and I opened the door and sneaked into the cold room to see a red sled with runners, partially wrapped and hidden for Christmas.

My mother's diary tells of one evening in 1937 when she stayed overnight at 749 after a long evening of bridge. Bill was away at the time; it was before they dated. She says that she had a great sleep in Bill's bed.

The third floor where we slept for those seven years looked tiny to us as adults. When my mother came to this house as a guest, first with Eleanor and then with Bill, she surely did not imagine that she would raise her children there, alone.

As we leave, we have our picture taken on the lawn in front of the house, my brother and I now in our mid-fifties looking much like our Riley grandparents did in that 1948 photograph. The house stands behind us, a reminder that our past is with us still, very much a part of who we have become. But today, the house holds fewer secrets as we leave it behind and walk down the driveway under the shade of the old oak trees and into the sunlight.